BODY LANGUAGE:

HOW TO ANALYZE PEOPLE, INFLUENCE PEOPLE, AND MANIPULATE PEOPLE WITH POWERFUL COMMUNICATION.

Charles Alexander Williams

Table of Contents

INTRODUCTION

Your body's language says a lot about you and has a significant impact on how others see you. You can learn a lot from other people's body language as such. When communicating and knowing others, understanding body language, along with verbal signs, can be useful. It can be exciting, but you are not a witch; you cannot read minds or understand what somebody thinks or feels. There is a technique to find clues to help you better understand and communicate with other people.

Psychologists are manipulating your body language as to how you feel and your mood. Even if you make genuine attempts to be real, your actions will tell you something else. But that doesn't mean that you're powerless. You can beat your body language by learning a little about your words and actions.

Whether you help people maintain their relationships, guide people for business success, or advise people on any other kind of issue, they see your body language; showing excellent listening skills makes people more comfortable.

People tend to communicate with each other. This can happen in ways that are apparent and not so obvious. We're talking, we're reading. We can also communicate without using words at all, though. This nonverbal interaction talks to our relationships when names are used to express information.

Our body language plays a significant role in the impression we create about our personality in people's minds. A good understanding of what messages we and others are sending out can help develop a better overall character.

CHAPTER ONE

What Is Body Language?

It only takes about seven seconds for the look on their faces to determine someone's mood. Body language is considered louder than talking directly. Many people can sense what mood you are in without even saying a word unless you are very good at hiding it. Your body's movement gives away how you feel, whether angry, sad, happy, etc. Your ultimate aim in relationships should be to be able to communicate appropriately. If your partner doesn't understand how you feel, not expressing yourself rightly can cause many problems. Human beings must express reasoning, solutions, and conclusions in ways that the listener is interested in or otherwise have no meaning.

Our bodies subconsciously send signals about our mood, emotions, and attitude towards people around us. You need to note how you use your body to determine what kind of messages you send out.

We knew terror, hunger, affection, rage, and joy by instinct. The body would show them through our faces, hands, and legs to express these feelings.

To decide how someone feels, body language is almost always required. If you've spoken on the phone to a friend or a loved one, you may have noticed that sometimes it's hard to tell if they're serious about something, joking, or even angry. This misunderstanding is the result of a lack of a visual language of the body. Your actions reveal more of what most people realize about you.

People tend to communicate with each other everybody does it? This can happen in ways that are obvious and not so obvious. We're talking, we're writing. We can also speak without using words at all, however. This nonverbal interaction talks to our relationships when names are used to express information. This is probably even more important than conveying the message. We're meta-communicating-about talking!

If words don't do it if we speak to an individual, we also need to explain how to interpret our text's content. The way we do this talk about this person's relationship, or at least the way we think about that person. Words are unable to do that. Showing is more comfortable than talking about our feelings. The meaning of our stories is the language of the through of the body. This language (in opposition to the parole) is used for nonverbal communication in the Saussurian sense. We're using it all the time. We don't even care about using it most of the time. Touching someone during the conversation means something entirely different than not feeling our conversation partner. Communication is not possible without the use of non-verbal language- the only exception is the written word.

Were we sure of that?

Most of the language of the body is unintentionally transmitted. Yet the value of our message is widely affected by it. We can infer that it would be good to become conscious of other people's body terminology and what is even more critical.

We could learn to use our body language for a purpose and understand other people's body language. They must also be aware of the cultural understanding of body language-its meanings that vary in different cultures. The definition depends on the other person's situation, language, relationship as well as gender. This means that not a single signal from our body has the same meaning in all parts of the globe. This is an important point that should be considered. Our body's language is integrally linked to spoken language or our whole pattern of behavior. With all this coming together, various stimuli can also complement each other to reinforce the sense of what they say. Many social groups have developed a particular body language that is very clear because, in a given situation, the use of words is problematic. Mostly these are minority groups in cultures where the dominant culture has a great history of prejudice.

Actions matter, In particular, body language is being used to express feelings. For example, when we love someone, it's often hard to directly say that to the person. On the other hand, it is easier to make our feelings clear through body language (intentionally or unintentionally). The opposite is exact, as well. We might say that we're angry through words, but our body language will speak loud and clear that we're NOT. This can be very frustrating to the message's receiver. Usually, the situation is defined as transmitting dual messages-one message in words and other body language news. Lying or covering up our emotions by body language is also problematic. By not being aware of their body language, we can give away their true feelings. Evidence has shown that many people pay more attention to their understanding of how a person behaves through the body's language than is through word and believes more readily. As consequences, we have to doubt the spoken word and question them if they do not adhere to the body's language.

Feelings matter

Awareness of how we interact= Important Only a small portion of how we meet another human is announced by the words we say (less than 5 percent, according to research). It is vitally important that we know our body language and regulates it (to some extent). Their body language receiver will have a sensation that is often hard to describe, put into words, or show that something has been communicated. But it's been. We've indeed all said to ourselves:' I don't think he/she likes me' or' I don't believe what has been said.' It is called instinct, and the body's language plays a vital role as it sends us information about the other person that we can understand intuitively. Firstly, we need to learn our body language. We should know about it so that both in others and ourselves, we can recognize it.

The Missing Ingredient

"What are you reading, my lord?" Hamlet said, "Words." Methinks he should have answered "body language." Where numerous are obsessed with words, we're always thinking about what we're going to say. Next, our body language is given relatively little attention. Strange since 55% of communication is transmitted through the body's speech, and only 7% involves words.

Take a moment to take reality into account. 7% of Words are communications. 55% Language of the body. It's a shocking fact, a fact that makes one thing clear: if you want to make the most of your communication skills— social, academic, or anywhere else— you need to use the language of your body.

So how could you take advantage of that whoppingly good 55% of contact that comes from body language today, right now? There's a lot of ways. Let's look at some of the most famous and important ones.

Conflict resolution: You may be one of the unfortunate people who often seem to get into arguments without much idea about why. Many people create conflict out of thin air. A confident guy who remains unnamed but serves as a perfect example gets into arguments regularly. He's thinking politically. He never says a word right, but he likes to get into debates. Why? Because the language of the body is anxious. He folds over his head with his hands. He rarely smiles, if ever. While he is talking, he will tap on a table or other item. His words remain polite, but there's nothing but his body language. The language of the body goes from annoyed to hostile to endlessly impatient.

This is likely the conflict's origin. Here are a few simple remedial measures and **will turn these** arguments into pleasant conversation.

Dating Body Language: Romance is probably the number one reason people care about the body's language. It's a smart step. In love, 55% of contact counts just as in everyday conversation in general. Using constructive and productive nonverbals can do an excellent job of presenting yourself as a desirable and, most importantly, open person. Here are some tips on how to target people by using nonverbal communication.

Don't smile too often, but give them a genuine smile when you encounter someone new to show you're pleased to meet them. Make that a habit. That way, when you meet someone you like, you're sure to give an excellent first impression, saying, "Oh, wow, I like you. I'm thrilled that we've met." Saying in words, this phrase means little, but when you say it through your body, it's a persuasive communicator, one that gets a relationship off to a good start.

Stand with your legs hip apart: some supposed specialists advise men to stand far apart with their legs to show dominance that attracts women. The question is that the guys are overdoing it. We turn a simple pose into their crown jewels ' comically fantastic spectacle. Just stand comfortably apart with your legs; this will show trust and strength.

Long Gazes: Nervous guys and girls will see a person they are attracted to look away shyly. Big error. It gives the impression that a) you're soft and b) you don't like the person you've looked at (because if you wanted to look at them, reason would dictate that you'd continue to do so).

Again, simple steps; little corrective gestures like this will make all the difference.

Let's look at one more field that is relevant for nonverbal communication.

Friendliness: Here are some tips to help you display kindness while still appearing dominant and solid through nonverbal communication.

Smile enough to let people know you're pleased, but don't overdo it. If you're used to fiddling with things and fidgeting with yourself, it makes the client feel you're fed up with them or annoyed with them.

Do not cover your neck, head, abdomen, or private with any barriers when you're standing (a wall may include your legs, a bag, an object you're holding, or anything else that gets in the way).

Point to the other person's foot and belly button, which shows a lot of trust in them. It's going to come across as a compliment and receive a lot.

These are but a few of the many ways you can affect nonverbal communication in your life. This chapter has explained how today, you could begin using simple gestures to improve your communication skills and build more positive relationships. Using them and see how much in your correspondence you find change. I'm sure you're going to be pleasantly surprised.

Helping to Understand Body Language

The language of your body says about you then has a significant impact on others see you. You could learn a lot from other people's body language as such.

Body language constitutes up to 55% of the way we communicate. Body language can indicate several different things depending on the context, along with verbal indications. People with powerful body language tend to feel more confident with free movements that take up more space. You are more likely to be less stressed, more dominant, more risk-taking, and more confident. The dominant language of the body creates a great look. Many studies show that faking low and high poses positively and negatively influences participants' confidence levels.

The impact of falsifying it until you make it may seem fake, but in forging it, the process will help you get it started with small changes in your body's language. Everybody can know something.

Here are three specific scenarios where the body's language is particularly important-a job interview, dating and catching lies, and ways to read between the lines to better understand what is going on.

We're just cheating a bit, like it or not. When we speak to a stranger, we are likely to lie in the first 10 minutes once or more. They might be little lies, but we're still doing it. Most of us will sometimes be interested in deceit to avoid conflict, but we're probably better off telling the truth. Words can be deceptive, but it's difficult for the human body to conceal lies. It can be instrumental in using your body language and reading other people's body language while interacting with others.

Body Language Basics: The primary goal when reading body language is to assess the level of comfort in your current situation. To determine this, there is a method of integrating verbal signals and body language.

Negative body language: moving from you or bending away legs or Crossed arms Looking out to side Feet pointing away from you or to the door scratching/ Rubbing their nose, ears or back of the neck A single signal may be deceptive

LYING: It is a significant advantage to judge if someone is lying by reading their Body Language. Your instinct is never 100% right, but when you've lied to you, you can become more conscious of practice. This method can help with the big lies, but identifying white lies, omission lies, and distortion are complicated.

Evidence has shown that liars also display a great deal of unpleasant behavior and other common characteristics.

Fake Smiles Research has shown that a genuine smile when pretending is almost impossible to falsify. That's why many people in family photos seem awkward. When they fake it, the smiles look awkward. Your real smile is in your face as your smile pushes up your cheeks, causing lines around your mouth. It's challenging to falsify that you need to feel a real positive feeling to do it, and if you're cheating, it's almost impossible. So a fake smile helps to determine whether a lie is going on.

Too much eye contact and a Rigid Upper Body Sometimes, with too much eye contact, a liar can overcompensate and look rigid when trying not to fidget. This can make you feel uncomfortable and awkward. People move in real interactions and do not have long-term eye contact. Liars are often rubbing their necks or ears because they're irritated, looking away to the side or choosing to do little. You are likely to talk to a liar when you note stiff shoulders and a high amount of eye contact.

Verbal Cues Pay attention to the interaction; if they are accused of something, the liars will give more specifics and suggest consequences for the actual criminals. They should answer your questions with a question that gives them time to respond. This kind of dialog, combined with the negative language of the body, leads to dishonesty.

Realizing that some people can always behave uncomfortably is essential. Search for several signals and trust your instincts and inquire if you're not sure.

DATING: It is incredibly helpful on the first date to consider the body language of your partner when not to talk about something that makes them uncomfortable.

You're only looking for general comfort and discomfort indications. It means paying attention to how the language of the body is covered. Many people will be relatively protected on a first date crossing their hands, keeping a distance, and holding their palms facing up. Your target is to encourage them to be more responsive and welcome you with uncrossed arms and a soft, genuine smile. We all want to mimic others ' actions, so if you're warm and comfortable, it's going to help them get more comfortable.

On a first date, comfort levels will fluctuate as they are anxious, and you are likely to make a few mistakes. Only keep going, don't worry. Search for the positive language of the body and focus on what it brings out. When you hear the negative expression of the body, the subject will change. Of course, when you don't jibe with the other guy, there will be evenings, and there will be many uncomfortable moments. Knowing the person wasn't for you and moving on if this happens.

JOB INTERVIEWS: Job interviews are close to the first dates except that you are on the same basis on time, whereas the interviewer controls a job interview. It creates a situation where the listener is more nervous than you are. You can easily show negative body language that you need to overcome to prevent being cut off.

First Impressions: First impressions count, so a smile, a handshake, and a warm greeting together with the aforementioned supportive body language bode well for a pleasant interview.

Go into the prepared interview, which will increase your comfort level and increase your level of confidence. To train the business and any individuals who may interview you for study.

Every fair interviewer will know you're a bit nervous and tense. When you are overconfident, it can indicate that you don't take the interview seriously.

In communicating and understanding others, understanding body language, along with verbal indications, can be useful. It could be fun, but you are not psychic; you cannot interpret or read what people are feeling or thinking about. Use this method to find clues to help you better understand and communicate with other people.

Speaking Without Words

Non-verbal body language is one of the primary forms of communication we use in our day-to-day experiences. It is the mode of communication that ignites the emotions and responses of our "good level." Studies have shown that gaining a body language understanding improves one's potential to succeed in getting out of any given situation anything one wants.

Have you ever looked at a lot sitting together and had a sense of how good or bad their relationship was in minutes? Have you ever wondered how easily, without any direct interaction, you were able to come to this conclusion? If you know it or not, we spend our days listening to the non-verbal signals of people being interpreted through their body language and concludes from our assumptions about them.

The body's language reveals the truth that we conceal from the world in words, including how we think about ourselves, our relationships, and our circumstances. The people we associate with can evaluate our motives, the nature of our relationships, how masterful we are in any given situation, our level of trust, and our true motivations and interests through our eye contact, movements, body position, and facial expressions.

In the emotional response it produces, the influence of body language is found. In nearly every situation, emotions influence decisions and reactions. Non-verbal signals activate emotions that decide an individual's core resources such as truthfulness, trustworthiness, honesty, skill level, and ability to lead. The perception of these signals will determine who we meet, the job we are employed, the level of success we achieve, and even those elected to influential political positions.

Why aren't we spending years studying and improving strong body language skills with such an extraordinary power? The truth is that most people underestimate the importance of body language until they seek a more in-depth insight into human behavior in a good relationship, or in a competitive market situation, they gain an edge.

Body language expertise provides people with the keys to perceive the context behind particular movements and body movement and understand how to convey and express messages while communicating with others effectively. As a result, there is a substantial increase in the overall success of interpersonal relationships. Understanding the basic understanding of the two core body language styles-open presence and closed presence-is, the best way to start this mastery cycle.

The closed presence body language style is found in individuals who fold their bodies around the body's centerline, running straight from the top of the head to the feet down the middle of the body

The signals sent to the world by the body language form of closed presence are a lack of trust, low self-esteem, impotence, and lack of experience. In extreme cases, it can even produce the message of wanting to be invisible. The consequences of this type of body language on the person projecting may range from actually not receiving the best possible opportunities to the worst-case scenario of harboring a self-fulfilling perception of victimization.

In comparison, the accessible presence is featured in individuals who create a sense of authority, energy, and leadership by projecting mastery of trust, achievement, strength, and ability. The physical characteristic is feet held apart, open hand gesture used in conversation away from the body's centerline, elbows held away from the body, shoulders held back, straight positions, and eyes focused on their listeners ' eye level. These people are seen as intelligent, successful, and attractive, quickly appear to succeed. We know this type of body language as the "leaders ' body language."

The aim is eye contact to enhance the body's language and begin projecting an open presence. One of the essential communication devices we possess is eye contact. You could change d way people view them by using direct eye contact when interacting with others. Once people start speaking directly in an individual's eyes, they are considered confident, trustworthy, and professional.

Hand gestures and facial expressions are the second transition levels with a transparent appearance that can be seen. Both modes of communication improve the ability to clearly and effectively convey messages. A more significant impact is produced through skillful expression when speaking by engaging the audience more visually and increasing the amount of information provided during the conversation.

As children, we are taught from an early age that good boys and girls are seated together properly with legs and hands folded before them. The desire to limit physical space as children could establish some of the characteristics of the closed identity in adulthood found in the body language.

To counter this effect, one can start adopting the aspects of the open presence's body language and incorporating these ways into their natural state of being. Completing this behavioral change will provide the same non-verbal experiences and signals as their counterparts in the open environment.

To establish the most powerful presence in all interpersonal interactions, the mastery of body language is vital. Individuals without this knowledge are susceptible to confusion and find their attempts insufficient in expressing their ideas. With the ability to differentiate between different body language styles, anyone can gain the mastery needed to succeed in whatever effort they choose.

CHAPTER TWO

Understand Your Body Language

Body language is an enormous variable responsible for how everyone you encounter comes to your mind if you know it or not. Listening skills are necessary to build good relationships with customers in many professions, particularly in occupations where you support others

Poor language of the body could result in you losing something significant. It's not that important to you! Listen carefully and honestly to each word. It's your body's language that makes other people feel secure, and you give them the attention they want. Understanding what a lousy listener's signals are here is crucial, and you should try to get rid of any of these. If you're in the habit of keeping your arms rolled up over your chest, or you tap your toes impatiently, lean or pull to turn away often, or while listening, you tell the other person you're not concerned in what he or she says. This will most likely result at the end of the partnership and can result in massive business losses.

So, what can you do to start sending positive signals from your body language to the person you're talking to? Next, try to face the other person in the square. To give a positive sign, don't look away. Then at the time of communication, we come to your body's pose. You must take an open stance. You never have to keep your arms or legs folded; otherwise, the other person would feel you're not interested in listening to his point.

When you lean forward while speaking to someone, your body's language says you pay more attention to what he or she says. Depending away, on the other hand, it means you don't have any interest whatsoever. Instead, we come to the touch with the ear. The most crucial factor is eye contact. Try to keep eye contact generally at all times. Whether you continue to look down or look away, it indicates you have no interest in the topic or feel uncomfortable. It is also not possible to ignore the significance of a relaxed posture. Try not to be too static. You should not be too formal when you speak to someone. If you feel you have suffered significant losses in the past due to your poor body language, then you should immediately begin to practice the above tips.

Body Language Talks All of The Time:

The moment you leave your home, your body language begins to speak for you. Even if you're not talking, how you're standing, how you're seated, and how you're using your feet, that's what others see as interaction. If you don't have a clear understanding of body language, your body language sometimes doesn't suit your thoughts, and people get the wrong message. If your body language contradicts your intentions, it could cause you a huge loss because you're going to lose your credibility.

How to maintain credibility:

So what are you supposed to do to keep your reliability? Next, we should know a little more about body language to be more trustworthy and professional in other people's eyes. Make your entry as positive as possible whenever you meet your customers for any business. How can this be done? As soon as you enter the client's premises, you should start talking about the company. Even if you have to wait a while, read any magazine instead is the best way.

Some More Important Tips on the subject of body language:

Another essential tip about body language is to warmly and firmly shake hands. Then we come to the choice of sitting on the chair. You should never say you're only going to sit when the other person asks you to.

You should instead select the most suitable chair and sit immediately. Never make the mistake of sitting too close or too distant from the customer, however. How much space should you have depended on the customer's personality? A private person will also want to sit at a distance beyond an outgoing person's reach. The vast range, though, is between 20 and 50 inches. When you try to put stress on any particular point, you can lean forward to get closer to the customer.

Effectiveness of Eye Contact and The Speech:

Another essential part of body language is eye contact. Eye contact, as well as a smile on a face, may send a message that you're a woman who is genuine, open, and honest. Vague eye contact and repeatedly looking here and there will send the message that you have no self-confidence. However, to avoid frequent look at the other man this will make the customer feel very awkward. Try to always talk with your normal tone. If your style is full of passion, will instantly capture the customer's attention

Body Language: What Different Postures Mean

Body Language: What Separate Poses imply The Tone of Voice is far more critical than the actual Words You Use Body Language applies to how you use the words instead of what you mean. If you talk in your normal tone, and the intensity is also in the normal range, your body's language can be outstanding. A very well-modulated voice with a regular rhythm and rate shows interest and passion. The phrases you use during your speech should be as straightforward as possible. On the other side, when using "um" or "ah" and excessively clearing your throat, it sends a signal that you feel anxious.

Concentrate On Posture and Gesture

Concentrate on stance and movement. You should also concentrate on your actions and postures if you want to improve your body language. Here are a few simple tips on how to improve posture. You should always walk openly with arms swinging, taking easy and determined steps, but you should stand up in an upright position. When you keep an eye on the other man, cup the chin between the thumb and the finger, or brush the nose bridge with your fingers, or hit the chin, then you're demonstrating that you're looking after what's being said.

Some Negative Indicators

On the opposite, foul body language suggests nervous gestures suggesting a lack of attention. All you need to do is avoid looking anxious and inform you about the body language message you are transmitting. For instance, if you fold your arms over your chest, cross your legs, try to pick up lint that's not on your clothes, or move your hands around your face, you're communicating your disagreement with the other person's point. Blinking your eyes over and over again, vomiting several times, turning away at the time of speaking, and rapidly moving your eyes to different places are indicative of a negative attitude.

Frustration

Anger When you point your index finger to something, your body language will indicate your rage. Similarly, tightening your hands, playing your hair, and firmly clenching your fists are also indicators of your frustration. Now, how does anyone prove he's feeling bored? If the listener's ears are not centered on the person speaking, if he's sitting in a wrong body posture or not listening to what's being said, he indicates he's getting bored. Once you encounter people from different cultures, the importance of body language increases further.

The Consequences and Benefits of Efficient Body Language

What more can you do with the dynamic language of the body?

Have you ever wondered what kind of knowledge your body has available, how important it is, and who can read it? Were you aware that there is now a growing interest in learning to understand this neglected field of human behavior? What are the advantages and disadvantages of this trend?

Productive body language supports productive organizations. One of the Information Age's main focal points was to streamline processes and make organizations effective. Hardly any company system has been re-engineered and scrutinized with the omnipresent use of spreadsheets and management software.

Although the introduction of machines and computers into our work and lives has saved a lot of time, energy, and anger, this primary focus on a technological solution might have made us go blind to the knowledge integrated and conveyed by our bodies. Our body language can and sometimes contradicts and even sabotages what is said through our well-rehearsed tongues. But how do you understand it when it happens?

For example, gravity's power and promise observe how significant the relationship with the average person's seriousness is. Most of us take for granted this immense power of attraction. Yes, if there are bills to pay, goods to sell, and people to please, who has time to care about gravity? Nevertheless, when it comes to holding our universe together, think about how strong the pull of gravity is. It even holds in place of our sun. Then you are welcome to marvel at the incredible amount of energy that many of us are using to resist this inevitable force. Only think for a moment about how much happier we would feel and how much more power we would have, how much better we can express ourselves by being a little more aware and functioning in line with the Gravity Force?

Most of us pay little or no deliberate attention to the performance level that we use to match our attitude with the pull of gravity. Since curiosity is an inherent part of human nature, it was only a matter of time before attention came back to benefit from more productive use of the body's language. What if the moment is here now?

Body Language Basics Learning Body Language Basics Take a walk in a busy place and watch your fellow human beings and use their stance to -Walk and stand on leaning backward, forward, or to one side, and operating against gravity.

Hang their heads clearly out of line with the center of gravity-Rock and wiggle from side to side as they step forward.

Move their feet in a different direction than that to which they move.

Wave your arms a bit more than just holding your balance-Shuffle so much when you walk that your shoes start wearing unevenly?

These non-essential movements require energy and effort to counteract the force imposed on them by gravity deliberately. Note also that small children use gravity most effectively, but we tend to ignore the pull of gravity more and more as we mature and become smarter. It's unnecessary and crazy to use one's energy to combat gravity if we use our resources efficiently. If we were blind to what body do when it came to our attitude, what kind of effect, unconscious or conscious, can this action have on those we interact with?

Pay attention to how most of us seem to be unaware of what our bodies are doing while we are going about our day. Many of these gestures are the product of our body language being subconscious or being conditioned to suppress it by society. Whatever the gain or effect, do something often enough and establish a pattern of behavior. It doesn't take long to become part of your identity once a design is in place. This pattern is ingrained for most of us into who we believe they are. Even with an injury, the system and muscle tension are often overlooked and linger if the initial pain you wanted to avoid disappears. Many go further by spending even more time and energy complaining about how tired they feel. Does this sound like our resources are being used efficiently?

Dynamic body language is often unnecessary knowledge that you are now invited to seek to warn somebody about your remarks. If you dare to take on this challenge, marvel at the answers you receive. Most will justify this politically, sometimes citing an old injury. Others will be offended to bring this up as this is "just the way things are." Remember how many warmly thank you for your advice and start to change these inefficiencies immediately. If knowledge is power, you often think that most others miss an opportunity to learn more.

Most importantly, you are invited to reflect on what body language, behavior patterns, and responses to your comments tell you about the individuals involved.

Do these trends make them more or less appealing?

Would you like to hire them more or less?

Are you interested in their suggestions more or less?

Do their age and intellect seem to affect how they respond?

Would you like to show somebody in your family these trends or to date somebody who does?

As a bonus, ask yourself what your response tells you about your ability to be curious, adaptive, and responsive?

What about your cues from the Body Language?

We've thought about all the other people around you so far. Here's your invite to stand in front of the mirror, take a reflective inventory of all the above questions, and see how they apply to you and the language of your body. What's your language of the body saying? How fast are you recognizing it and adjusting it? By the way, how many people around you might know how to read it as well?

There's a gold mine here waiting for those who understand how to read, feel, and interpret what another body language is demonstrating. Those who are conscious of what their body language is telling are also waiting for a jackpot. Those who realize that they will feel healthier and happier by changing theirs will become more desirable and successful are waiting for a third jackpot. Could the language of the body have anything to do with your success?

How long can you manage to stay unfamiliar with body language?

Present the book Sensational Presentation Skills Consciously!

For 20 natural and sensational soft skills, click on the link below to drastically improve your ability to "transform" your listeners into practice. Whether you want to lead better, sell better-helping others, or develop more team spirit learning how to communicate more effectively is necessary. Here's a chance to have fun learning how to speak in public.

Body Language In Sales Market

They all spend a lot of time listening in the selling skills classroom-not just doing it, but doing it, and appreciating that focused, structured listening is often the one that disturbs even the best salespeople. Yet listening is not about our hearing organs alone... We also have two faces and are perceptible even more than our looks. Yes, our eyes can read details that words are often unwilling or unable to communicate. Our knowledge of body language-that' uncanny' ability to read and interpret the facial and body's subtle signals is vital to our listening post in the selling and negotiating environment. It can both shield us from danger and lead us to an opportunity: it can be both Sales Tool and Sentinel.

It is often more reliable than verbal communication because body language is stimulated by our subconscious and remains largely unconnected to our deliberate expressions of feelings. It may even refute what is said and serve as a detector of lies. It is used in areas such as law enforcement for that very purpose. Quick, can quickly lose almost indiscernible motions of the head, ears, and mouth to an untrained observer. These so-called micro-expressions, or bursts of reality, are impulses that are too impulsive for the conscious mind to process. Such glimpses can provide vital perspectives within a fraction of a second. They may reveal covert reactions to happiness, sadness, and surprise, or may reveal distracting concerns such as frustration, anger, and fear. In the blink of an eye, it can expose even efforts to hide intensely formed feelings of distrust, disdain, and contempt.

To detect these, police interrogation officers have long used the tactic of placing the interviewee under intense light with at least two witnesses in full view to ensure that they can' see' the truth. It has become common practice to have expert observers on hand to interpret body language signs in court proceedings or review video footage. Since it would be naïve to believe that there are no lies, half-truths, or pretense in the commercial world, it should come as no surprise that body language also has a crucial role. Perception of these micro-expressions can undoubtedly give an unfair advantage to buyers and sellers, just as they do for serious poker players and professional interviewers.

In culture, it even plays a key role. Good comedians typically get their best laughs by delivering intentionally, but embarrassingly, punch lines that are out of step with their facial and body expressions.

Even if they are confident with their lines, they still struggle to overcome disagreements if their natural style or personal opinion causes body language responses that are out of sync with the script needs or clash with the director's delicate nuances.

This is one of the most challenging aspects of their learning. While we understand that the face and body language come from deep within, and we acknowledge that it is mostly unconscious, it is still tough to master it with any real consistency.

The simple task of crossing our arms is a simple illustration of this. Each time we do it the same way, usually left for right-handers over right. When you tell us to reverse it, you need to think a little bit. Some of us find it challenging to do. Start it now and see how you're going. And once you've done it' unnaturally' knowingly, you can be sure that the very next time you cross your legs, you'll find yourself doing it the same old way.

Body language is not structurally different from our verbal language. To give them context, actions are usually combined into clusters or sentences and can be quite unreliable when read in isolation. For example, rubbing our hands together in tandem with other signs usually signals excitement or hope of good things to come, whereas it can mean nothing more than we're cold and trying to heat our hands on our own.

Interestingly, we know and appreciate most of the common signs and can show them on command when prompted. Children play happy face / sad faces from a very early age, and most adults can win the occasional charades game. So we are not overwhelmed by the simple dictionary of symbols. We seem to know all of them once we've been told. I do a straightforward exercise in my lab sessions to illustrate this.

Every student receives a single word card to define an introductory phrase, such as fear, doubt, acceptance, distrust, contentment, etc. Everyone is called to carry out the expression at random, with the others in the group needing to remember it without prompting. Over-acting is allowed, and all too popular is an exaggeration. Everybody attempts to communicate their message to others through various physical configurations, often more imaginative than in the real world.

It seems that we all have a reasonable vocabulary in body language, and all we need to do is to raise our awareness. We have to recognize its importance, then train and prepare ourselves to watch and interpret the signals at all times. We have to observe the change in particular. Each of us has a specific physical style, from the nervous retirement individuals ' timidity to the overly confident's boisterousness. We need to detect any deviation from the norm in the buying and selling situation, particularly the apparent indications showing a change of trust or a hint of untruth.

I urge my trainees to remember my home-grown axiom-' Gaining insight through detection is a far better option than allowing deception to be monitored.' There is no substitute for training, and if playing charades with your partner every night gets a little bit, try watching a small TV with the volume turned down low, then switching the sound off entirely as you get a better grasp of the story. Even without the ability to read lips, most of us can discern enough from the movements to follow in silence a typical action movie.

You're going to be an expert in no time with a bit of commitment, but just a word of warning here for all the males among us-no matter how well you do this, you're going to play catch-up with your female colleagues forever. I'm a big believer in injustice, but the fact is that males in this department are not the same as their female counterparts. Without doubt related to motherhood's physiological demands to naturally understand a newborn baby's needs, women are far better equipped than men for this. We seem to have that so-called sixth sense. The signals are much clearer to them, giving them an authentic edge in the stakes of intuition, particularly in the deeper waters of feelings and trust.

Some can't believe what they've overlooked in all the day-to-day activities they've been playing out before them' invisibly.' The body language topic consistently rates as the most valuable contribution through the course assessment feedback from the live sessions.

Since any reasonable study of body language deserves much more coverage than I can give it here, I can only draw your attention to some of the main features and offer some suggestions about what general areas to look into. I hope this isn't too little to confuse you, but enough to inspire you to go much further with this subject. To build a framework for this thrilling endeavor, here are the main categories of the face and body language that participants explore, behave, and strive to refine in my live workshops: Regions and Zones- each of us has a personal space that differs according to what we're used to.

Unwanted infringement of the personal zone of the other person can intimidate and become threatening in the extreme. On the other hand, it may seem unfriendly to stay too far away. There's a very old expression-a bit extreme, but very unforgettable-' If you're going too far into the personal space of someone else, it's best to either kiss or kill them.'

The invasion of space also has residual and transitory elements. For example, we' own' the seat we've just been sitting in public places. We indignantly assert our position in the queue and generally adopt a squatter mindset based on prior positioning or use. We seem to be stakeholders in our claim to a private territory wherever we go and what we do. Therefore, being responsive to the part of another-real, presumed, or historical-is a critical social capacity.

Palm motions-these These are obvious signs, and we can make a lot of observations. An open or upturned palm generally means openness, invitation, and friendship, whereas a downturned palm is usually a sign of demand or superiority. A clear example of this would be someone who leads others to their seats, where the arm extended with an upturned palm would be seen as an invitation to take a chair compared to a downturned palm that would be taken as a seat directive. Variations of the closed hand, or fist, usually show agitation, annoyance, or even anger; finger and thumb extensions may provide even more visual signs, from the extremes of "pointing a finger" to "giving it the thumbs up."

Hand/arm movements are daily, ranging from an uplifted hand signaling stop to a clenched fist showing anger to hands, forming a contemplative steeple. Arrows held behind the palm-in-palm back indicate authority, an example that you may have noticed in various news reports showing Royal Family members, military leaders, or senior politicians inspecting the parade troops. Subtle hand movements to different parts of the head, such as mouth, nose, ear, and eye, have very distinct meanings, ranging from lying to boredom, and will often provide an apparent and easy-to-read contradiction of the spoken message.

Arm and leg barriers— blunt arms crossing in front of the body and close leg crossing usually sends a hostile or defensive message. Using the arms or legs more overtly as a shield usually denotes vulnerability. We need to be careful not to jump to conclusions, however. Can misread Loosely-crossed arms as an isolated gesture. It's the most natural and calming way to sit or stand in some situations, yet we still tend to read it negatively. To be safe, we need to look for other signs of support.

Face signs-from the gaze of a surprise to the downward look of thoughtfulness, to the side-looking of doubt, we all know these. More subtle movements of pupils can even anticipate the next move of the other side. For example, they're reflecting on something up to the left; as the pupils move up to the top right, they're planning how to act on it. Pupil size and positioning are often sufficient, but in combination with widening or narrowing the eyes and raising and lowering the protective brow, our eyes have their language. For instance, we agree that a genuine smile is one of the most disarming and infectious expressions that we can make, but the face, not the mouth, will subtly reveal whether the smile is fake or real. At the other end of the scale, thinning or pursing the lips may merely indicate thoughtfulness, but when the brow falls towards the nose, the eyes roll up intensely towards it, we see signs of concern, maybe even anger.

Have you ever noticed how animated films, just simple cartoons, convey feelings? Take a close look the next time you have the opportunity-it's all in your eyes. Yes, it's said the eye is the soul's window. There's no more accurate word, whether we're bargaining, arguing, selling, writing, or just plain romancing.

Voice signals-some of these things have been discussed earlier, so look for accentuated shifts in voice and inflection and be very mindful of prolonged pauses. They need to watch and listen, as these vocal changes appear to suggest that should include visual stimuli in the deal. For example, a speaker will often intentionally pause for effect without a telling facial expression to qualify their position and direct your answer.

Ownership signals-we must be attentive to signs that signify a property that is coveted or forbidden. Have you ever seen a photograph of a young man with his car in which he does not lean on it or touch it in any way, or a young bride clutching her own husband's hand-or the bridegroom embracing his bride affectionately to show the world that she is his? Ownership gestures are critical in our selling and negotiating situation, and like territorial issues, they can have a historical component.

First, in the early qualifying stages of a purchase, the previous or current owner of a brand will show much of the customer's desires and wants, likes and dislikes, and should be a key questioning line. One of the most graphic of all purchasing signals at the closing stages is where the consumer starts owning the product, making it digitally by moving closer to it, holding it, even wearing it, or trying it out.

Ownership is not just about physical things either; in a discussion or debate, it is just as important. We will send subtle signals to indicate acceptance as others come round to our way of thinking. Classic' knowing' signs like nodding and contemplative head-tilting can show us clear signs that they are starting to take control of the idea. We mustn't miss these essential purchase signs across the sales desk or negotiating table; they can be real game-changers, not just time savers.

Copying and mirroring-we often ape their movements or positions if someone creates a favorable impression on us. Hands-behind-heads in the seating position are a prevalent example and a (mainly) male gesture to signal approval and justice. The yawn is, without doubt, the most vivid illustration of the unconscious and contagious essence of mirroring. When we see someone with a mouth ajar or even catch a stifled yawn, it seems like we can't help ourselves. Having our customers mimic our position and gestures in our sales setting is a good early indication of partnership-although;

From our side, by mirroring the other party, we can create powerful nonverbal suggestions. Modern studies of hypnotics' power in marketing show that making ourselves look more like our client reduces consumer resistance and makes them more receptive to our tips and advice in conjunction with our corresponding conversational techniques.

Body reduction-the formal courtesy of bowing is no longer standing in a modern culture outside countries such as Japan but can still see informal signs of respecting the form of head-nodding and hat-tipping. Even in today's cultural environment, lowering the head remains a symbol of submissiveness. It is, however, still evident, not as pronounced in adults as it was in childhood. For example, people entering a room where a meeting is in progress will' stop' back to their seats; an unconscious attempt to avoid interruption is to lower their profile.

Use pointers-pointers, like pens and pencils or our hand, can be used very quickly to draw a person's eyes away from a screen or website back to ours by tracing the motion. This is a valuable tool for avoiding distraction and is used to control eye contact by experienced presenters. Even the body itself gives us helpful signals, particularly our feet, pointing inevitably to where our mind is going.

Seating arrangements-the positioning of barriers such as counters and desks can denote power play. The best option for ready and honest discussion is the full vision of each other. For example, the arrangement in a meeting room can have a real impact on participants ' ability to engage. Experienced presenters and negotiators are very careful to adapt the seating configuration to the ideal meeting environment.

They will often find ourselves in a triangular configuration in the open showroom sales atmosphere about the three focal points-our clients, the service, and ourselves. Keeping it this way and not getting between the consumer and the use is crucial. We need to avoid circumstances that present barriers or uncomfortable conversational settings in the situation of trade selling. Sales representatives calling retailers and traders often face the problem of conducting the sales interview in the middle of a showroom or worksite. A much better option is negotiating an office or meeting room's quiet corner to allow full and uninterrupted visual communications.

They also refer to the "negotiating table" in the negotiating context. Okay, but unless we set out to exploit the degree of engagement and

60

cooperation intentionally, let's make sure it's round. Having a round table discussion' is more than just an expression; a round table invites open and fruitful discussion without long and short sides, edges, corners, or barriers.

Listening Begins With Your Eyes

People have much more to communicate with than words. More than 60% of what people share is not spoken at all but shown in their body language to be seen by all. Most importantly, whereas the words which people that may often lie, body language at all times tends to tell the truth. If you want to know what people are doing, you have to start listening to what their bodies are saying with your ears.

Thousands of books on body language have been published. They try to explain the sense behind every physical move away, sit back, lean forward, cross your legs, and even scratch your nose. Okay, it's a beautiful and astonishing hypothesis. But if we understand what the body wants us to say, we need a better tool than somebody motions list and what they tend to mean.

A technique that codes a person's body language as blue, yellow, or red is the best decoding body language.

Green body language means your listeners are open to your words and interested in your idea. Green body language involves active eye contact, head nodding, leaning forward, free hands, laughing, and the audience approaching the speaker, but is not limited to.

Yellow body language suggests that something is on their minds for your listeners. They're frustrated with what you're doing for whatever reason, and until you deal with anything that triggers the yellow signal, you're not going to connect.

Red body language means that listeners don't care and don't want to hear. We are either angry and upset or scared and nervous. Red body language suggests that if you keep pushing the point, you're in danger of causing a misunderstanding, so you'd better fix the relationship before moving forward. You ignore a potent signal and make a bad situation worse when people turn their backs on you, and you keep talking. Red body language involves, but is not limited to, forming a fist, moving away, shaking ahead, personal space violation, avoiding eye contact, flapping arms, frozen postures, and any sudden or aggressive gesture.

Now, I bet you know at least one car driver who behaves as if a traffic signal's colors have the following meaning: red, stop; green, go; yellow, go faster.

To beat the red, have you ever sped up for a yellow traffic light? Most significantly, have you ever torn through the yellow body language of someone to make your point?

Usually, when people see yellow body language, they rush forward with their logic instead of slowing down and allowing their listeners to catch up. Even the most visible body messages are overlooked, crashing into conflicts, ramming into misunderstandings, and asking why no one ever listens to them.

This person's ability to read and respond effectively to body language also dictates the difference between socially-advanced people and socially-inept people. Many people read body language incredibly well; however, only a few can respond to what that body language communicates quickly and effectively.

We continue to press forward with our words while people's signs quietly call for us to yield. Someone is turning away from us, yet out of the room, we are following the man. Someone is raising a hand to us, but we are expanding our voice and steaming forward.

If we don't respond to body signals intelligently, we create communication issues everywhere. If someone sends you green body signals, it means you are linked and talking, so you should feel free to continue speaking.

However, if somebody gives you yellow body signs, you must slow down and create understanding instead of chatting. You were in danger of colliding with a belief, tearing into an idea, or crashing into an ego, if you hurry through a yellow signal, so slow down and create green alerts. You can always make your point later when, once again, the person you connect with is open and concentrated on what you have to say. If you're waiting for a green signal to continue, you'll be much more likely to make your point because the person you're talking to listens.

Finally, signals from the red body indicate the relationship has collided. You'd better stop it all and get it back off. Give them the space to navigate, or you're both going to sink. Give them some leeway before they cool down and start sending green signals back to you.

CHAPTER THREE

Body Language Interview Techniques

Did you know that giving every interviewer a strong resume or curriculum vitae nowadays does not necessarily guarantee you are landing the job? You might also be able to answer all the focused questions correctly; however, if the body language sends the wrong signals and messages throughout the interview, you will still not be close to receiving and signing the appointment letter.

It may come as no surprise for many. Still, statistical data have also shown words have only succeeded in contributing 35% of the message being transmitted. In comparison, your voice and body language tone command 65% of what is communicated.

Just by looking at your body language alone, an experienced interviewer can access the nature of your characteristics already. Whether you're a confident person or not, whether you're the open and friendly guy or the shy and quiet man, whether you're a team player or a solo loner, or whether or not you're honest and genuine. The interviewer will pay attention to what you say during the question-and-answer phase and carefully analyze how you say it. You will then look for all those comments, reactions, and answers from you that suit their requirements for the offered role.

If you put it in your mouth, body language will show your true feelings to the interviewer. If you are without the knowledge or awareness of your negative attributes from your actions, you definitely won't be able to get on their right side. Signals and movements such as anxiety, fear, weariness, dullness, dishonesty, and lack of integrity can potentially project your lousy image and lose you the job application.

It is difficult to overemphasize the significance of body language during the first four or five minutes of the encounter. In comparison, soft and awkward handshakes will only transmit a half-hearted message that will only undermine and degrade an otherwise optimistic situation.

Start seated only after the interviewer has told you to do so. Simultaneously, be aware of your surroundings and stop having to face a bright and shiny window, as this will make it difficult for you to maintain good eye contact. Try not to be afraid to ask or demand politically for a seat change if you have no opportunity or preference to stop the sunlight glare.

You will need to put yourself in a positive and relaxed way to start in the right direction and avoid projecting any negative body language patterns. Ensure you always have space for yourself to shift and reposition if you happen to be restless or rigid. Meanwhile, secure yourself in a comfortably seated upright position to ensure no part of your body under any pressure or strain, especially from the neck area.

Raise your head to the same eye level as the interviewer to display an engaging smile while at the same time relaxing your back, but not to the point of slumping to the floor. Place your hands on your lap loosely or place them on your chair's armrest. By doing so, you can use hand movements at any moment to help what you say to clarify your comments and make the conversation more interesting. The interviewer will look at you as confident and comfortable with the interview's progress with hand gestures that support your words. Bear in mind not to get too excited and result in overdoing in excess the motions and actions. This will project only an awkward shape that indicates anxiety or hostility.

All the necessary and useful body language movements and signs you must always be mindful of during interviews are described below: Using Your Voice Power Successfully* Express confidence and excitement through your voice's firmness.

- Don't pinch too hard on your face. High-pitch voices are challenging over the years, making you sound like a whining child.

- Avoid enthusiastic gabbling and mumbling because no one trusts a speedy speaker.

- Vary the conversation voice and dynamics, so avoid talking too loudly or too softly.

- Talk slightly slower than usual to keep your presence smooth and steady, but don't overdo it.

- Always pause to avoid unconsciously responding and having the wrong words coming out of your mouth before beginning the next story.

- Test your tone range to prevent dreary and weary monotonous speech.

- Negative Body Language Behavior and Habits to Avoid* A fixed or distracted look indicates that either you're dreaming during the day or your mind is somewhere else.

- Hesitating or looking away before or during your speaking time indicates you're unsure what you're doing.

- Constantly rubbing your eyes or mouth while talking means you're deceptive or hiding something.

- Doodling on paper shows that you don't pay attention and that you don't care.

- It's irritating, distracting, and a sure sign of boredom to click your foot continuously.

- Arms folded or crossed suggest a refusal and a reluctance to listen.

- Constant fidgeting suggests frustration and restlessness.

- Good postures and gestures* Attentive: nodding, grinning* Listening: verbal recognition, nodding, tilting of the head, constant eye contact* Responsive: open arms, leaning back, nodding harmful postures and gestures* Lying/deception: glancing around, rubbing of the ears, averting of the eyes, hands over the mouth, awkward shifting of the chair* Aggression: clenched fists, cutting hands.

- Don't fidget when you feel uncomfortable when you're sitting. Slightly change your position and sit up straight to keep an alert.

- If you are faced with a difficult question, stay calm before answering and be aware of your negative body language patterns. Stop jumping into an unpredictable expression.

- Watch and mimic the movements of the interviewer. Postural and gestural echoes bring together, and you will receive a more precise answer.

- Relax to create a relaxed and comfortable look. Do not hurry through the interview; simply flow the pace and let the interviewer set the pace.

- Keep eye contact consistent and alert, but try to stop looking from time to time.

- Smile expression can give positive emotional reactions. It will restore your enjoyable nature and enthusiasm, but be mindful of senselessly over-delivering.

At job interviews, body posture and movement are vital ingredients. Through our facial expressions, the sound of our voice, and also our eye language, our emotions and inner feelings are easily conveyed to the interviewer. Ensure that you always sound relaxed and optimistic by speaking with a calm, consistent, and managed voice that can be easily heard and understood. Thin and soft voices do not seem to have the vital energy and do not inspire others' faith.

What you want to do here is to focus and use your body language to define your abilities, qualities, and values to maximize the interviewer's potential.

Take some time before the actual interview day to practice and rehearse using the role-play technique with a family member or a relative. Note that it makes training better. You will protect half of the job before you even enter the room when you are well trained.

You always have to consider one final thing, as this is the most critical aspect of any job interview. Be on time and arrive on time. Being late is to say goodbye to the conversation more or less before it even has an opportunity to start. There will be no company interested in employing a person lacking in professionalism and corporate ethics. Being early by an hour is much better than being late by just one minute.

Your Body Language Speaks Volumes About You

The language of the body speaks volumes as a man within you. It is the number one factor that determines whether you can catch the attention of an attractive woman or whether you can blow it out absolutely. I've already written about how to use your body language to attract women. Now I will discuss how negative body language can impact your dating / social life. Some of the body language features you may have will be highlighted that hold you back in your search to pick up women. Imagine the setting to be a nightclub for all these scenarios.

You see a woman tempting you. She sits at a table alone. With long steps, you get up and begin to walk towards her, head held so that you seem to look down on people. You get to her plate and look down at her there. First of all, long steps show that you are in a hurry, and women do not see this as self-control. There's a difference between walking with your head held high and keeping your head so low that you look down on people. Another shows self-confidence and a sense of self-worth, and the other depicts a guy who seems to think he's better than anybody else. People see this as selfish and want nothing to do with self-absorbed people. One of the something worst is to do is to tower over and probably startle an unsuspecting woman. You're showing the woman that you're a bully, and you're seeing her as an object by not sitting down and being her equal, not to mention that in the process, you've insulted her. It all ends and starts with your body language when you see a girl you want to approach. From the moment you get up from your chair to the moment you hit it, all people, including those that attract you, are watching and judging you. If your body language is unfavorable, you will not achieve positive results, and you will be assured of rejection.

Are you one of the shy guys sitting alone watching any girl entering the club? Once you see a girl interested in you, you have no idea how to handle her, so instead of putting yourself through' the solution ' pain, are you trying to convey your message by looking at her? It's not a good thing to do to start a girl. This makes them

75

uncomfortable, just as if someone looks at us makes us guys uncomfortable. This evokes a woman's reaction to a' fight or flight.' Think about it this way: what result do you get when you look right in your eyes at a strange dog? The dog gets very agitated, starts to bark, and if bound, he will likely try to break it to get to you. Staring is an aggressive form. The' fight' will be a harsh rejection, and the' ride' will be her leaving the club because you've just made it too awkward for her to stay. When you look at a woman, she will see you as hostile.

The next one is something I've heard every woman talk about in my social circle, and it's the number one activity that will not only get you rejected by women but can also get you out of a club. Women call it' party stalking.' I saw it myself, and I saw the effect it had on every woman in the club. I'm going to give you the scenario in which I saw myself as an example of the very negative and terrifying form of body language. A few weeks ago, I was in a club with a couple of lady friends and found this guy standing on the side watching one of my friends, and we're going to call her

Samantha. He stared very intently at her. He also noticed it and figured that he was just one of those shy guys who didn't have to touch the nerve. She got up to go to the bathroom, and I realized the guy was gone. She was distraught when Samantha returned to the table. Not only had this man followed her and stood within viewing range from the washroom of the women, but he also followed her outside and quietly observed her sitting against a wall as she had a cigarette. I looked up to my right at this point in her tirade and saw the same man leaning against a wall about fifty feet away, glaring again at Samantha. I glanced around the club and found that a couple of other people took little peeks in his direction, possibly because he was also watching them. Samantha was frustrated with this guy because he was so insecure in his body language and actions that she felt insulted by him. Without even saying a single word, he had earned her contempt. Samantha told me that sometimes women run through this kind of guy in a club, and the whole reaction is,' Please don't touch me.' She also said some women would get the bouncer to take them to their cars and wait for their cabs with them. Such guys are afraid of women as they likely ought to be. A vocabulary of the body resonates with aggression. I was indeed in a fight or flight mode myself on that particular night. If I'm in this mode as a man, what effect do you think this will have on women? Trying to get a woman is a terrible technique. You could get a' pity' dance with one at the very best because they're too scared to say no. You're going to be kicked out at the worst.

It is the biggest turnoff for women to have negative body language. If you ever want to get to the' approach' level, this needs to be fixed immediately. Women won't give the time of day to men who look like bullies by towering over them, almost daring to reject them by a woman. Our very feelings about bullies are that they are likely to talk a bit with our hands with their wives, so denial is a guarantee. Ogling women or robbing them of their eyes makes them unbiased. It's not artifacts. We are people. You're not going to attract any girl doing this. For all of you guys out there who think it's a turn-on for people to' stalk' girls around clubs to demonstrate their attraction, quickly lose the attitude.

No one likes to be followed around, man or woman. This invokes a state of battle and flight in both. It's the number one turnoff, and it's probably going to get you booted from the club or in a confrontation with someone because a woman who feels threatened is going to grab a bizarre guy to block you. Some guys are women's security, and they want to deal with you on a personal level. All these critical aspects of body language are a severe obstacle to women's access. Such characteristics have to go, and they have to be replaced by more supportive body language before you even think about approaching a woman.

Nevertheless, not everything is ever lost. To see what kind of person you are and what kind of man you want to be, it just takes practice and a look inside. Of course, the rest will follow.

Nonverbal Communication is the Message

Nonverbal communication is the meaning that our body language passes between individuals, such as facial expressions, head movements, body posture and acts, clothes, mannerisms, personality traits, etc. You've probably heard that 55% of our communication's overall impact is determined by our body language (nonverbal communication). The sound of our speech decides another 38 percent. And the words we use (verbal communication) choose just 7 percent.

Many similar actions in our body language have been found by researchers to have specific meanings.

Face, facial movements, and motions, for example, provide data on the type of emotion being expressed; body position and stress indicate the strength of the feeling.

One language of the body that I find in people is the face's grimace as they listen to someone who tries to communicate or describe something.

That's quite rude, and it's as if they're saying, "Come on, can't you tell it fluently," "Why do you have such a hard time talking," rather than just waiting patiently for the person to speak in the best way he/she can.

Another kind of illustration of body language is someone dozing off during a lecture presentation; it says something about the respondent's feelings towards the session, the speaker, or the business— either the presenter is boring, or the participant is entirely disinterested and rude.

Caution is needed in all of this analysis of body language. Too many people will read a book or take a body language course and begin excessive criticism of others after the test.

Just because a book says that "crossing the arms over the head" is a symbol of superiority or uncooperative, it doesn't mean that everybody who takes that stance is transmitting that message. Not at all.

How many times did you do it and wasn't uncooperative? Perhaps, this pose is simply because one is tired of having his / her arms hang from the sides during the long, drawn speech of someone! It's a comfortable location. Sometimes I do it without any negative meaning.

I saw some of the most positive people in the conferences, listening attentively to the speaker, being most accommodating and pleased with what the presenter said or did— all with arms crossed over the head!

Another common topic in body language is about the speaker's eyes shifting around the room intermittently while speaking. This is meant to mean a few things. I even saw listeners look up to the ceiling because there was a momentary focus on the speaker's eyes.

Several experiments have gone so far as to suggest that the eyes' position also indicates what data they are "fetching" wherein the brain (i.e., left eyes, right-brain scan, right eyes, left search, left search, etc.).

I noticed people looking at one corner of a room while talking just because there was a diversion!

There is a lot of truth to it in the right-brain / left-brain system, but sometimes "experts" may get too carried away. No one yet knows all about the mind.

People are "searching" for their feelings most of the time. Interestingly, if you observe, you can notice that people intermittently lose eye contact while speaking but concentrate while listening steadfastly. Most of us are doing this.

Nor does disconnecting the listener's eye contact necessarily mean that the person hides something from his listener— or lies as some "expert" tells you. Sometimes they can do that, but they don't do it more often. Those findings are the outcomes of the study of extreme behavior.

Nonverbal communication is the meaning that our body language passes between individuals, such as facial expressions, head movements, body posture and acts, clothes, mannerisms, personality traits, etc. You've probably heard that 55% of our communication's overall impact is determined by our body language (nonverbal communication). The sound of our speech decides another 38 percent. And the words we use (verbal communication) choose just 7 percent.

Many similar actions in our body language have been found by researchers to have specific meanings.

Face, facial movements, and motions, for example, provide data on the type of emotion being expressed; body position and stress indicate the strength of the feeling.

One language of the body that I find in people is the face's grimace as they listen to someone who tries to communicate or describe something.

That's quite rude, and it's as if they're saying, "Come on, can't you tell it fluently," "Why do you have such a hard time talking," rather than just waiting patiently for the person to speak in the best way he/she can.

Another kind of illustration of body language is someone dozing off during a lecture presentation;

it says something about the respondent's feelings towards the session, the speaker, or the business— either the presenter is boring, or the participant is entirely disinterested and rude.

Caution is needed in all of this analysis of body language. Too many people will read a book or take a body language course and begin excessive criticism of others after the test.

Just because a book says that "crossing the arms over the head" is a symbol of superiority or uncooperative, it doesn't mean that everybody who takes that stance is transmitting that message. Not at all.

How many times did you do it and wasn't uncooperative? Perhaps, this pose is simply because one is tired of having his / her arms hang from the sides during the long, drawn speech of someone! It's a comfortable location. Sometimes I do it without any negative meaning.

I saw some of the most positive people in the conferences, listening attentively to the speaker, being most accommodating and pleased with what the presenter said or did— all with arms crossed over the head!

Another common topic in body language is about the speaker's eyes shifting around the room intermittently while speaking. This is meant to mean a few things. I even saw listeners look up to the ceiling because there was a momentary focus on the speaker's eyes.

Several experiments have gone so far as to suggest that the eyes' position also indicates what data they are "fetching" wherein the brain (i.e., left eyes, right-brain scan, right eyes, left search, left search, etc.).

I noticed people looking at one corner of a room while talking just because there was a diversion!

There is a lot of truth to it in the right-brain / left-brain system, but sometimes "experts" may get too carried away. No one yet knows all about the mind.

People are "searching" for their feelings most of the time. Interestingly, if you observe, you can notice that people intermittently lose eye contact while speaking but concentrate while listening steadfastly. Most of us are doing this.

Nor does disconnecting the listener's eye contact necessarily mean that the person hides something from his listener— or lies as some "expert" tells you. Sometimes they can do that, but they don't do it more often. Those findings are the outcomes of the study of extreme behavior.

Dare to Experience the Real Teacher

As common as the topic of body language learning is becoming, what if a crucial point still ignores 95 percent of what is currently being discussed?

Brilliant people from social and behavioral scientists to psychologists and actors are now, understandably so, advertising themselves as body language specialists. As they talk, we all show the effect of body language. Roughly everyone now acknowledges that you are at a disadvantage if you miss important cues, from flirting to negotiating complex contracts. You accept the following, though?

TV, reality, or reality of television?

I'm trying to point out somebody's language indication just about every time I do a lecture, seminar, or some private coaching. Whether it's for a team or a single person, I'm going to show what they're doing and then suggest something more useful. Nearly everyone then does it politely, and most people usually look happy with the outcome. They go back to their old routine 30 seconds later. But they quickly return to their comfortable and familiar place just like watching a TV show, as if what just happened was a business break. We respond to business as usual, regardless of the effect on their health and communications efficiency. Does this also make you wonder whether we are creatures of habit, as many philosophers have argued, or are we responsible human beings capable of controlling, modifying, or mastering our behavior?

Dare to feel the difference that makes your Body Language!

It becomes increasingly clear after researching this trend for many years that those few listeners who choose to alter their behavior specifically actively are those who hope to experience a difference. They allow emotionally to touch them with the suggested adjustment. Everybody else seems to have gone through the motions politically. Some of them often seem to have detected something, but they quickly return their attention to the activities (instead of the emotions) and prevent long-lasting changes. They seem to respond automatically, to put it another way, as you would by touching a hot stove with your hand. We have no difficulty calculating the difference, but they have to avoid thinking that nothing else is being achieved actively. Could this subtle difference be the key one that distinguishes those who only gather more information about body language from those who seek to think, understand, and master it?

Dare to Understand the Real Trainer. This distinction also seems to distinguish most of those who now teach body language methods from those who concentrate on communicating a warm and sensational understanding of their work with others. Indeed, body language can be an intellectual exercise, and there are currently several healthy, well-meaning, and well-thought-out demonstrations. We still write body language analytics systems right now, aren't we?

You can teach others to learn and change your body's language just as you prepare for a math or bee spelling exam, but how do you handle all that extra knowledge? No matter how good you scientifically understand various movements and patterns, the moist and moving aspect of feeling can easily miss the effects. What if this clear yet essential distinction of deliberately daring to relax and think distinguishes well-meaning, well-trained human activities from an open and growing community of responsive and connected people?

So here is both my contribution and invitation to this fascinating sector. I'm committed to mastering body language training so you can feel the difference in acting. To do this, you can count on me to keep developing new, sensational soft skills. Soft skills allow you to feel the difference and become aware of what every cell in your body is saying, quickly, effectively, and enjoyably. Tools that encourage you to learn, think, and hear how every little move you make affects how you feel and how you can influence how others think of you.

Welcome to the road where you feel every little change you make to see if you're getting closer to or further away from a safer, happier, more efficient way of being. The goal is to know precisely how to change your body's language to feel more confident, healthy, and connected regardless of your circumstances. Through cracking this code, your desire to have fun would make it exponentially easier to draw more of what you want into your life and work. What's the future going to look like, and the role you choose to play in it?

CHAPTER FOUR

Accurate Body Language Interpretations of the Way You Walk

Do you understand that perhaps the normal speed walking of the average male is three miles an hour? And if we were lucky to be okay not to be immobilized in our lives physically, we would all be able to walk and continue to walk from the age of two until we split this life. It is possible to learn some insightful hints about a person's character by watching how they walk. Several criteria are associated with the way a person moves when he or she walks.

Mood, Levels of fitness, emotion, and type of body play a significant role in contributing to a person's movement's different kinds of steps, posture, and pace. An individual's movement behavior can be acquired primarily from the family, along with other prominent features. Typically, it will be quite obvious the next time you have the opportunity to watch people walking in groups, different posture, and expression among family members.

They usually have a springing with a lightness in their steps when happy people are walking. Conversely, with a hunched stance, a depressed person can walk and gradually pace with heavy feet, while a fast pace and upright posture imply a confident person with a clear sense of direction in life.

Please remember to take into account the context and atmosphere when watching the walking pace of someone. This differs from country to country, from culture to culture, and from town to state. For example, due to the vast difference in general lifestyles, the pace adopted in a dense and populated city would undoubtedly be much faster than a small town in a suburban area. Posture is still known as a very reliable indicator in most situations.

1. The Folded Arms Walk During hot or warm weather. walking while the arms are folded usually suggests that a person is a defensive and protective mode. This explains as well a lot why most women take on this pose as they walk alone in a crowded street full of strangers. Some people even take the same pose when feeling insecure in an unfamiliar place.

Whether the arms are tightly crossed, gripping the chest, or even loosely wrapped around the body does not matter. These arm positions are the direct evidence of the confusion, fear, anxiety, and lack of confidence. These gestures, supposedly self-hugging, are the way the individual gives himself physical reassurance.

2. Hands In The Pockets Walk. If people put their hands in their pockets, it essentially means they feel cold at the time, mainly when it's a cold or windy day. But when placed in the sense of a person's characteristics, this usually indicates a very private and introverted person. This person conceals from the outside world his or her feelings and personality and yet at the same time can be other people's cynical and judgmental.

Sometimes he or she walks with a lower head in combination with a draggy and inconsistent pace. The adverse movements made here reflect a person's depression. And if from the very start this depression is driven by frustration, it will include a lot of jumping on small objects on the floor in the walk. Even the imaginary ones are sometimes not excluded.

3. The Deep Thoughts Walk. People who think deeply about something when they walk will show their heads bowed and often look at the ground with their eyes unfocused. The motion here may indicate that such people have anxiety, but they're only strolling to focus on their thoughts.

That stance will seem disconnected from others because the people here do not want any distractions from anywhere to stop the attention at that moment from their sincere thoughts. Walking up and down in deep thought walk will be a widespread practice of this loss. And the real goal here is not to reach any specific destination but to conclude.

4. The Strutting Walk. The strutting posture is relatively rigid and inflexible, and the chin is usually raised to display a superior and proud image. People strut traditionally walk with chest forward pushed in the arm movement combined with an exaggeration.

This walk's logo has a unique way to show the person's confident, arrogant, and selfish character. The goose-step marching military parades is also known as a ritualized form of strutting, superiority, signaling, control, and signals.

5. Hand on Hip Walk. Walking with one hand leaning on the hip-bone while moving their pelvis forward is a position often used in fashion shows by catwalk models. This seductive pose is described as a form of sexual body language that models use to enhance the garment's appeal.

Many women like to adopt the pose when flirting with men as it could effectively call attention to their erogenous zones, making them look sexier. On the other hand, it will seem unmanually and sissified if a person embraces this. Homosexual men usually combine this gesture with a feminine gait to express intentionally in a very conspicuous manner their inner sexuality.

Should you take small steps or significant steps in life? How comfortable is your pace? Look at the sky, the ground, the houses, or other people as you walk? Everyone has a distinctive way of moving, but how do you usually walk yourself is the crucial question here.

This might come as a surprise to many, but you knew that if you walk with a relaxed, upright posture and confidence, people around you will respond more positively. The explanation is that when you walk with an erect posture, your body will be more upstanding. You will also be more observant and sensitive to your surroundings, giving you a more accurate assessment of what is going on around you.

Women and Their Body Language

Perhaps the ever-mysterious definition of body language is one of the most fascinating and yet confounding aspects of dating. While it is necessary to consider the variations from individual to individual, many standard features can be an excellent way for a potential suitor to proceed if read correctly.

Positioning: When a woman spots a potential romantic interest in a social gathering, she often starts a series of subtle maneuvers that allow her to be placed in the direct line of sight of that interest. Depending on the physical features she wants to present, she chooses the right seat or position and often takes note of the lighting's particular effect in that area.

She wants to show herself while waiting to attract her chosen interest to decide what a woman feels. Low or open seating is often the favorite of those women who want to display their legs, while women who are self-conscious about that feature often choose a seat where their legs are hidden.

Hair is often rearranged unless it is already styled in an immovable way; once a woman finds her attention and this fine hair playing along with even a moment of eye contact as an invitation to approach.

Most women are fully aware of what they consider as their physical flaws or strengths, and they will choose to put themselves in a position that flatters both. An example of this might be the difference in sitting position between two women; one of whom is proud of her abdominal area, the other who feels she is out of shape in that particular region of the body: one woman may choose to allow this area to be glimpsed, a subtle display of stretched position that may even reveal a little skin, the latter, being more self-conscious, will choose to hideth

One of the most critical aspects of positioning is how the woman is engaged in conversation or some event that will allow her to observe her interest without considering the person too much. Many women find a more direct approach to enticing. They will continue to make their look clear without removing any of the more subtle signs, but, as most people fear rejection, it is much more common for women to proceed with acts that seem to have nothing to do with attracting attention.

While the particular gestures can read these and many more subtle signs of invitation, rejection symptoms are just as significant. Often, when a woman has no interest in her potential suitor, she may demonstrate both facial expression and body language outwardly. She no longer wants to engage with that person in conversation or action. The action of folding arms is probably the most common and well-known, an almost sure sign that something is wrong with the person. If eye contact is made, a lack of eye contact or a purposeful look away can be a sign of dismissal, although sometimes this action can be caused by embarrassment rather than lack of interest. The intentional positioning facing away, putting the suitor on the back, may also suggest a lack of interest; this gesture eliminates the suitor from view and indicates that the suitor's actions are incompatible with the lady.

The Walk: However, graceful (sometimes not at all), many people have another way to walk that can quickly reflect their moods or unconscious intentions. In particular, it is possible to read the swinging of hips and slow, languid motions as a sign of interest. Typically women tend to move in more gradual and more deliberate ways when they have found a person close to them that they find desirable. However, one might still be unsure which person is the subject of interest; when a woman moves in this way, a potential suitor must remain watchful for more indications that their advances may be welcome.

Distress: Women tend to slouch under stressful situations, close their eyes (especially when brought to tears), and generally move in sudden, awkward movements. Although this may indicate that an approach is unwanted, this is not necessary; in fact, many women use the act of "damsel in distress" to attract potential suitors. Even nowadays, where gender equality is a much-discussed and thought-out issue, most women still take on more feminine cliché traits when attracting a suitor. Should not view such behavior as a sign of weakness as a sign of uncertainty about handling an interested person. Suppose a problem arises by physically showing the symptoms of stress, and the suitor is attracted by coming to the lady's help and offering to help. In that case, we can avoid the awkward approach entirely as the two people start discussing the issue.

Touch: When engaging in a conversation, there may be many gestures that signify attraction; a mental pat on the back or a nice bit of the hand may be subtle ways that suggest a woman's feeling relaxed and mutual interest. Until attempting to approach or converse with a woman, however, there may be subtly touching items in her atmosphere that serve as mock touches of the person she is interested in. Some of the more open and well-known of these encounters have a lot to do with the eyes. One can always presume that physical attraction and intervention are welcome and practically necessary when eye contact is made during these acts.

The Smile: Although the sense of this facial expression may seem evident on the ground, following it is by no means a standard "green light." The smile of a woman can be an invitation or only a friendly dismissal; before making assumptions, one must always try to read the signs of the rest of the body language. Placing the eyebrows in a high, arched position, coupled with a smile, is an example of a smile that is nothing but an invitation to a potential suitor; this gesture is more often a sign of rejection, disapproval, or irritation, and if detected, one should proceed with great care.

An arched brow combined with a smile can be a tricky expression to read, and in this situation, when attempting to discern meaning, one must look to other parts of the body.

A smile that is supported by the lowering of the lids is more frequently and a sign of genuine joy, whether induced by amusement or desire; one can usually rely on this expression to suggest that an idea will not be ignored, although perhaps not yet sought.

Such body displays used to attract another individual's attention are not often prepared or even contemplated when walking around or positioning yourself in a room. The instinctual desire to use the body as a lure is often acting naturally after thousands of years of instinct and the many social behaviors acquired by our culture to show certain features that one feels are attractive and attract attention. Paying attention to this kind of body language can be an excellent way to see if the lady accepts a suitor's approach and can help prevent hurtful or awkward rejections. Although not an exact science, a lady's subtle displays and acts can sometimes show more in only a few minutes than hours of conversation; knowing the signals gives you a significant advantage in both the dating world and perhaps even in a relationship's future.

Tips for Reading Woman Body Language Signals

Would you like to hear what she thinks and feels? How to decipher the expressions in her body language to get it right. It has never been easier to understand her body language.

1. Her coffin. A pink flush can color her chest's skin as she plays in the foreplay; this is known as a "sex flush." This is due to changes in blood pressure and metabolism, as well as breathing and heart levels. This is her smart way to tell you that if you keep up with what you're doing, you could get lucky. Another positive sign that you're doing it right is when you start to expand your breasts. Women's breasts, when sexually aroused, will rise by as much as 25 percent.

2. Her schoolchildren. The eyes of a woman will dilate if you stimulate her. Her brain is subconsciously made to want to see more of what visually pleases her. The irises have to let in more light to do this. She also starts looking hotter at this stage, as research has shown that guys are more attracted to girls with larger pupils.

3. Her eyelids. Look for a minute in her face. She must blink about fifteen times a minute. Evidence has shown that women blink 32% quicker on the Pill than those who aren't. How's that benefiting you? Girls on the Pill are more sexually attracted to guys with rugged faces and strong large jaws due to the change in their hormone levels. Strive for the picture that is calm, strong, and intense.

4. The little back of her. She's going to start arching her back as a woman nears orgasm. Clasp her tightly around her waist and be careful how much she's doing. Now, don't stop. Keep going before she hits the climax. It's coming to you.

5. The eyes of her. The first thing in the morning is the sense of smell of a person. You might want to clean your teeth when you feel caring. The first thing in the morning to cook her meal is the perfect way to impress her with your cooking skills. What's the reason? Because the scent is 90% of the meal's flavor. Because it has a scent that enhances the blood flow to her vagina, hot banana bread is best if you have love in your heart.

6. The fingernails of her. Clear signs of anxiety or depression in women are body-focused repetitive activities such as nail-biting or cuticular picking. Remember not to stop nagging her; this can only make it worse. Try to take her hand, squeeze it gently or rub it, and then continue to hold it.

You could sense the pressure leaving her side.

7. Her feet. Warm head, cold feet. Looks like she always has cold hands? Research shows that her hands are more chilled than yours, at least 3 degrees. Once anxious, it falls even further. The bodies of women are conditioned to keep their core body temperatures colder than their legs

8. Your brain. The brains of women react to alcohol differently from the minds of men. Whereas men lose their alcohol inhibitions, women tend to be more sedate. You can turn up the music if you want to get her in the party mood. Mid-to-fast music is going to put her in the spirit and make her feel more sociable.

9. The ovaries of her. When she ovulates, female sexual motivation is at its peak. It happens two weeks after the end of her cycle. She's most libidinous when a woman's most fertile. Cautious.

10. The skin of her. When a woman begins to play with her hair, she sends strong signals that she is accessible in the sexual body language. Stroking her hair is a good sign, but the hair flip is the best of the lot. It is said to be the best indication she's drawn to you sexually.

11. Her chest: Striking her neck or playing with her necklace are also unambiguous flirting signals of the body's language; she draws attention to her breasts by doing these things. Throats and necks are the only areas of the lover, and the message is even more vital when she arches her neck.

12. Her mouth: she covers her mouth when a woman begins to think about sexual thoughts. Licking her lips, chewing suggestively on the straw or fork, or sticking stuff in her mouth are all signs she might be up to. Faster feeding, drinking, and cigarettes are also fantastic expressions of sexual thoughts in the body language.

Use the skills of your observation! Learn these cues from body language to seduce your partner.

Conscious Body Language and Powerful Sales Training

Could sales professionals stay at the top of their game without their sales training using intentional body language?

When it comes to human growth, marketing managers are pioneers.

It would help if you continuously adapted to what draws your clients and regularly change what repels them to remain at the sales profession's forefront. The concept has never been as relevant as it is now. Gaining confidence from today's sophisticated consumer is the biggest challenge facing skilled salespeople with the abundance of information available to customers.

Gone are those days when a salesman (yes, mostly men) would be able to crack a dirty joke, pull out their order book (yes, paper) and book a big sale with a fat margin. Your potential customers have access to the same information as you in today's competitive market. The disparity between your opponents and you have vanished in their minds. Even using the most advanced CRM program has little impact as something is going deeper. The marketing pendulum is now swinging back to the value of a relationship of trust from many years of nonpersonal business transactions. These days the trend suggests that people get tired of been treated as numbers on sales. People are gradually voting with the wallet to be regarded as independent and distinct individuals with corporate social responsibility. Would you blame them for that?

Many of the cutting edges is talking about the value of creating and maintaining hot and trusting customer relationships, from Forrester Research to Harvard Business School. Wise leaders are now taking steps to train their staff as a trusted person to handle every customer. It is also essential that we now need to teach people how to view others as human beings. But how can this cycle grow without paying more attention to body language's importance?

Sure, even body language becomes more relevant. This is excellent news, but what if there is yet another level separating elite sellers from the perfect ones? That's becoming mindful of your body language and using it effectively with emotion. Understanding how to shake hands properly, when to lend your pen to get a signature, and when to open or cross your arms is one thing. But what if it's a separate and hitherto ignored dimension to start connecting these and many other movements with the feelings and atmosphere they make. The more you understand and know what's going on with you and those around you, the more comfortable and graciously you and your customer will be able to dance together on the way to your next sale.

Some ideas for promoting this cycle and becoming more mindful of it at the body language level are:-Salespeople become more present as they instinctively vanish into their sales presentation. It still seems more natural to forget how you interact with someone who needs to be seen, heard, and understood. The more you can practice juggling being here and now with your need to know where you're in your sales cycle, the sooner you're going to succeed and the less you'll have to accept returns.

You are attentively listening rather than just waiting to speak. Until you answer them, actively pause and reflect on what your prospective client has just said. When you finish their sentences for them, they'll sound as if they're speaking to a computer as a fellow human being. Using all your senses and trusting your instincts more are both criteria to hear your potential customer's whole story while adding value to the career you have chosen.

Serve your way to selling, rather than moving, delivering, and impressive. Relax, ask questions, listen carefully, and respond in a way that feels special to your potential customer. The more unique they think, the more they respect you in general. Know the causes of emotion — train to reflect and respond more while responding less automatically.

It is making your goal more accessible and desirable. The more deliberately you change your body language to communicate with your audience, the easier it will be for them to graciously decide to do business with you over and over again.

To maximize the conscious body language, each of these points requires a new set of soft skills. Such skills could create a more aware and current relationship where you and your potential customer can relax and expand your shared respect and understanding. The effect will be a better negotiation structure, less cognitive dissonance, a longer, more stable, and friendly business relationship with fewer returns.

Arguments for bulletproof marketing and consumer capture, not!

As the difference between products, companies, and sales tools narrows daily, this traditional selling way is becoming less and less effective. Customers can change vendors faster than you can create new marketing claims with the massive over-supply of rivals in just about every sector. Human nature is what it is; life is still easier for everyone when discovering that you are a trusted supplier to their clients. Seek to become someone who is sincerely interested in long-term partnerships rather than merely making the next offer.

The current trend in establishing trustworthy and loyal customer relationships is how to conduct future business. The more you learn to hear what your body expresses, the more you can adapt and change your message to respond effortlessly to your customer's needs, expectations, and wishes. What if selecting a trustworthy manufacturer, this genuine and sensational array of soft skills quickly becomes the decisive factor? Training your organizational and social sensitivity in this exciting new phenomenon will help you develop your edge.

You are attentively listening rather than just waiting to speak. Until you answer them, actively pause and reflect on what your prospective client has just said. When you finish their sentences for them, they'll sound as if they're speaking to a computer as a fellow human being. Using all your senses and trusting your instincts more are both criteria to hear your potential customer's whole story while adding value to the career you have chosen.

Serve your way to selling, rather than moving, delivering, and impressive. Relax, ask questions, listen carefully, and respond in a way that feels special to your potential customer. The more unique they think, the more they respect you in general. Know the causes of emotion — train to reflect and respond more while responding less automatically.

It is making your goal more accessible and desirable. The more deliberately you change your body language to communicate with your audience, the easier it will be for them to graciously decide to do business with you over and over again.

To maximize the conscious body language, each of these points requires a new set of soft skills. Such skills could create a more aware and current relationship where you and your potential customer can relax and expand your shared respect and understanding. The effect will be a better negotiation structure, less cognitive dissonance, a longer, more stable, and friendly business relationship with fewer returns.

Arguments for bulletproof marketing and consumer capture, not!

As the difference between products, companies, and sales tools narrows daily, this traditional selling way is becoming less and less effective. Customers can change vendors faster than you can create new marketing claims with the massive over-supply of rivals in just about every sector. Human nature is what it is; life is still easier for everyone when discovering that you are a trusted supplier to their clients. Seek to become someone who is sincerely interested in long-term partnerships rather than merely making the next offer.

The current trend in establishing trustworthy and loyal customer relationships is how to conduct future business. The more you learn to hear what your body expresses, the more you can adapt and change your message to respond effortlessly to your customer's needs, expectations, and wishes. What if selecting a trustworthy manufacturer, this genuine and sensational array of soft skills quickly becomes the decisive factor? Training your organizational and social sensitivity in this exciting new phenomenon will help you develop your edge.

CHAPTER FIVE

Public Speaking Tips - Control Your Body Language

Your delivery body language is probably more important than the words you're using and how you're putting them together. If your body language is non-existent, aggressive, or defensive, it will represent your audience's feelings. If your body language reflects something other than what you say, the audience is unlikely to believe a word that comes out of your mouth.

Unconsciously, most listeners ignore what they hear in favor of what they see. Getting an optimistic and robust body language and a confident attitude will, therefore, make the audience feel you are an expert, believe you are trustworthy and know what you're talking about.

You have to keep in mind five places for using body language in presentations: Posture-your posture should be visible as soon as you enter the building. If you're waiting until you're in front of the crowd to move to a position of trust, you're too late. Your audience's opinion starts to form the moment they see you first, whether it's in the parking lot, the elevator, or even the restroom.

When you got up and took the front of the room from your seat, show trust and purpose. Stand with your head held high, keeping your chin parallel to the floor with your feet hip-distance apart, which will lengthen your spine and make you look bigger. Take a moment or two to stand still at the front of the room before you start your presentation, making sure you have everyone's attention.

Gestures and Motion-The Gesturing aims to make your presentation lively and enlighten. Management tends to explain and magnify critical concepts, which ultimately lets you understand what you're saying. Since there is a lot of visual perception and retention, movements play an essential role in making this happen.

There are four standard sizes of gesture-gestures that only include the fingertips are called small movements. Gestures that pivot on your wrist are small. Motions that hinge on your elbow are considered significant, and gestures that originate from your shoulders and travel outward, upward, or downward are considered extra-large. To be visible and impact the audience is, the more significant the movements need to be.

- Open-handed gestures build more confidence and relationship (comprehension) with your audience than closed-handed gestures. You subconsciously assume that you have nothing to hide when you're audience can see your hands.

- Do not cross your body's midline with your arms as this builds a barrier between you and your audience, so you appear defensive. You also want to avoid pointing out that it can be considered threatening or that you accuse somebody.

- Just walk when you're moving to a new idea you want to share with a friend, like walking at the start of a sentence. Take only three steps at a time while walking on the stage. You need to match your eye-contact, hand, and leading foot all together when taking these three moves. Don't be shocked to make you look confused; make purposeful your gestures.

- Do not sit on it or get stuck behind it if there is a podium.

- Do not turn your back on the audience. If when you stepped forward, you need to go back to where you were standing, move back discreetly on a diagonal, and step back slowly as you emphasize key points.

A facial expressions-The genuine smile is the most potent, all-purpose expression of the face. A genuine smile can include the muscles of your zygomaticus that are the ones that cause the eyes to grin. A pleasant smile will reassure you and your audience, so try to practice this one in the mirror before you hit the stage.

The way we use our eyes and facial expressions can have a tremendous impact on our appearance. When it comes to eye contact, you want a touch with your eyes that is not too long but not too short. Too quick eye contact occurs when you watch the audience watch you, while prolonged eye contact can make the person feel uncomfortable.

Look for clear eye-to-eye contact at a time with one man. The best time to use eye contact is between 3-6 seconds. Use your eye contact to provide you with suggestions about what the crowd feels like. Whether they follow you or look confused or bored, you can change it appropriately. Body language is used to deliver an excellent presentation; it is about understanding and improving the audience along the way. A facial expressions-The genuine smile is the most potent, all-purpose expression of the face. A genuine smile can include the muscles of your zygomaticus that are the ones that cause the eyes to grin. A pleasant smile will reassure you and your audience, so try to practice this one in the mirror before you hit the stage.

The way we use our eyes and facial expressions can have a tremendous impact on our appearance. When it comes to eye contact, you want a touch with your eyes that is not too long but not too short. Too quick eye contact occurs when you watch the audience watch you, while prolonged eye contact can make the person feel uncomfortable.

Look for clear eye-to-eye contact at a time with one man. The best time to use eye contact is between 3-6 seconds. Use your eye contact to provide you with suggestions about what the crowd feels like. Whether they follow you or look confused or bored,

Another mistake people make when giving presentations is to look at regions in the room instead of the people. Make every effort to bind your eyes to others, as the show is not the place for them.

Dress–Choosing a professional look allows the audience to see you. Since the way you dress sends a message to your audience about how much you value them, it can make or break you. Choose things that make the audience feel you're interested in them.

Dress to make a memorable impact in the best possible way when making a presentation, but don't overdo it, as you never get a second chance to make a first impression.

Sexy Body Language Tips for the First Date

You're with your dream date on your first date. Signals from the body language of sexual to show you they're warm for you. Flirting tips for a successful game of dating.

1. Look, worshipfully. We all have trouble changing our attention when drawn to someone. Even when our desire object has ceased to speak, there is still a lustful look. Use this to your advantage to be a little suggestive, and keep your eyes on your date at the silent count of five during a talk break. In comparison, the more often blinks your partner, the more nervous they are.

2. Hold your hands. Nervousness and tension indicate a clenched fist. Worse yet, whether their hands cover their heads as it means utter exhaustion, or they're about to fall from tiredness or alcohol. Those who are nervous tend to hold their own hands and fidget on the table with objects. Hands freely placed on the table with palms facing upwards suggest an open person more comfortable. Aim to loosely place your hands on the table if you're incredibly nervous, as this gives you stronger vibes than putting your fingers together or folding your legs. When talking, putting your hands on your chest makes you look vibrant and honest.

3. Speak size. A voice will not be too high or too low when they make you an equal. Deafening sounds appear to belong to dominant personalities, and to the meek, they are very quiet veer.

4. Autoerotic touch unconscious. For several reasons, sexy thinking leads us to touch ourselves subconsciously. First, to pay attention to different parts of the body. Second, we're touching each other to taunt the other. Second, blood rushes through engorging extremities while sexually aroused, making it super sensitive. Then it feels good to move.

5. Boyfriend. A decisive move in the sexual language is when your date starts eating, drinking, or smoking faster. You get to open your mouth when you think about sex. Putting things in your mouth means you're sexually interested. Women eat ice cream cones, run and suck their fingers with spoons.

6. The hair of her. Interested girls are going to start playing with their hair. Fluffing her head, stroking her hair, and the most important of all, the hair flip, are all accessible or flirting body language signs. When she starts hiding behind her head, however, she displays disinterest.

7. Guys fiddling. We start giving off their flirting signals as guys become sexually excited. These may involve scratching the nose, playing his band, running rings over his fingertips, or fiddling in his pocket with loose coins. It is a sign that he wants to look good for you to change his hair.

8. Check your butt. If you catch your date by checking out your ass when you're leaving the table to visit the bar or bathroom, you'll have lustful thoughts.

9. Stripping symbolically. All strong sexual body language movements are loosening ties, undoing buttons, pushing up sleeves, and removing jackets. Mother nature's way of making us naked with someone we share sexual chemistry with is openly undressing without knowing it.

10. It's touching. Where does the date go uncertain? Try the test of touch. Touch your side, your leg, or your shoulder. Unless they're shy, if they like you, they will return the contact in 10 minutes.

On a successful first date, three sets of touching should be available every time for three seconds.

11. The glass of wine. The date is a winner because he rubbed with his fingertips the rim of his drink. Similarly, when she runs up and down her bottle. She certainly flirts if she also makes direct eye contact and plays with her straw. Wine glasses kept at or above chest height; however, are a warning that a second date will not happen similarly if both hands were wrapped around their glass by your date.

This is a significant body language unconscious check to gauge the first date. Deal with an object from your tableside, e.g., wineglass, fork, etc. Lean back slightly and quietly pushes it to the side of the table on your date. Remove your arms, lean back, and continue to talk. If your date takes it back to you, you won't be interested in it. If they leave or hold it where it is, you're lucky. Move another entity on its way and leave the hands on the table to take it further. The romantic date will now also lean forward and move something over to you from their side of the table.

12. Kiss, kiss, kiss. All these definite signs that date is open to a kiss: licking the lips, touching their mouth, bringing their head next to yours, seductively eating and drinking, and tilting their head while looking at you. Begin the kiss on their lips with a soft light comb. You should stop if they pull back, clench your lips, or slap your face! If they're leaning over, they're happy to continue with their mouths or touch the back of their heads.

It has never been easier to flirt by nonverbal communication! Use this body language dating advice and give your sexual signals. Flirt to a second date on that first date!

Begin the kiss on their lips with a soft light comb. You should stop if they pull back, clench your lips, or slap your face! If they're leaning over, they're happy to continue with their mouths or touch the back of their heads. It has never been easier to flirt by nonverbal communication! Use this body language dating advice and give your sexual signals. Flirt to a second date on that first date! Begin the kiss on their lips with a soft light comb. You should stop if they pull back, clench your lips, or slap your face! If they're leaning over, they're happy to continue with their mouths or touch the back of their heads. It has never been easier to flirt by nonverbal communication! Use this body language dating advice and give your sexual signals. Flirt to a second date on that first date!

Leveraging Change Management And Entrepreneurship With Conscious Body Language

A crisis of trust is rooted in need for more entrepreneurship and agility or death. From the internet's well-known business specialists, you can have the best change human resources and investment tools available. However, if you don't feel and radiate confidence as a leader, you will still found you and your crew in the growing seas of uncertainty.

IBM and other IT firms ' sources of confusion have sold billions of dollars in hardware and software by playing management ambiguity. We recognize that by growing feelings of fear, doubt, and remorse, we can pay out large sums to lower risk and feel safer. Nevertheless, if their salespeople do not express genuine faith, the chances of selling themselves and their goods will decline rapidly. It is confusing to fear the unknown. The more you think you can predict what's going to happen, the more confidence you're planning to manage. One of the keys to can confidence is your ability to break down significant unknowns into smaller components that can be handled. It allows you to put the confusion on a tangible handle. It will also help to look forward instead of behind.

The physiological mechanics of trust Another area that needs to be addressed is the body's conscious language and its effect on your level of confidence, ability to decide, and lead others. What if you can take advantage of your ability to inspire and engage others by merely adjusting your stance and breathing more? What if your confidence is a feature of the congruence between your feelings, words, and deeds?

Ideas This what you believe affects what you express, and experience is now almost widely accepted. Positive thinking is a good start, but combining this with a positive feeling will dramatically increase your confidence. Smiling is a simple way of increasing your chances of feeling lively. Are you aware that regardless of whether you change a few muscles on your face or have a warm and fuzzy heart feeling, smiling would release endorphins into your bloodstream that encourage well-being and healing? Take a moment to relax and see if you're not beginning to feel better. You extend that to those listening, too, if you feel better. During the cycle, you become more attractive.

Words What you feel and then say often affects your ability to build trust. If you're nervous, your eyes tend to focus on what might go wrong or the mistake you've made or believe you're going to. The words you're thinking and using are going to be more harmful. Cells are talking to each other not only in your skin but with those around you in coats. If you focus on a dubious conversation, it will be felt by those around you. On the other hand, listeners can also believe that if you rely on a positive outcome.

Terms and interactions can either be compressive or detailed. The conditions you choose to think and convey influence your cells to concentrate on either growth or defense. Lively conversations cause your cells to open up, expand and share more of what's going on around you, and ultimately you. Negative interactions will facilitate the closing and compression of your cells for increased protection. Will then transmit the defensive message to your body. In short, that old childhood rhyme of "sticks and stones breaking my bones, but names never hurt me" was not as accurate or comfortable as we have been led to believe.

Deeds The breathing and posture have a tremendous influence on how you feel. Compared to a high and straight TV building, how much trust does a potato sack radiate? Look around the people around you and see how appealing you find them and how straightforward their attitude is. Do you want to exude more trust? Then get straight! Deeds The breathing and posture have a tremendous influence on how you feel. Compared to a high and straight TV building, how much trust does a potato sack radiate? Look around the people around you and see how appealing you find them and how straightforward their attitude is. Do you want to exude more trust? Then get straight!

Would you like to inspire those you speak to? Let's start from where the inspired word comes from. Initially Latin, it means "breathing of spirit." Take a long, deep breath of inspiration. How does that affect why you feel? It doesn't matter how good you felt when you feel a little better now. We're just virtually wind instruments. The more oxygen we encourage our lungs and voice boxes to move through, the more words we say can resonate with our cells. Increased resonance is calling for increased confidence. Why do you think there is a deep, dark, vibrant voice in the most popular radio and TV announcers? Because it encourages us to have more faith in them and buy whatever they sell.

The more you practice aligning your feelings, words, and language of your body into one corresponding message, the quicker and more successful you are to deliver it. There is an apparent lack of committed leaders in our current world of instability. It is a great bonus to become more aware of your body and its language to distinguish them from those trust artists who have learned to use their body language to deceive. If you want to drive others into a brighter future, become more agile. Get more awareness of your message with your body. Making it something we all look forward to thrilling and inspiring. There is an apparent lack of committed leaders in our current world of instability. It is a great bonus to become more aware of your body and its language to distinguish them from those trust artists who have learned to use their body language to deceive. If you want to drive others into a brighter future, become more agile. Get more awareness of your message with your body. Making it something we all look forward to thrilling and inspiring.

Conscious and Innovative Body Language

Successful creativity is impressive as it blends the best of smart thinking by communicating it in a way that "moves" others into practice emotionally. That mix is often a challenge because many young, technological innovators prefer to focus more on innovations, technology, and devices than individuals. The sales and marketing styles prefer focusing more on the consumer than on the mechanics of what they offer. Very few seem to be reasonably well suited and doing both. And, for those who do,

I had the privilege of working with many IT and Telecommunications companies regarding their management, marketing, and presentation skills. From that experience, I can tell that magic starts to happen when technicians relax and become confident about the power and leverage available to interact actively using their body language.

I've found that the most popular wake-up call for innovators comes when they get a clear picture of how much knowledge their bodies transmit, whether or not they know it. A brilliant idea often doesn't leave the PowerPoint slide because either the listeners are irritated or put to sleep by its delivery. To achieve the next step, the quality and delivery of your message must inspire and attract. You might invent the ultimate mousetrap, but if you cannot deliver it in a manner that encourages and stimulates your audience, who are you speaking to? An appealing thought to consider, for instance, is how the world would look now, he had encouraged himself to build. While he seems to have been self-expression (witness the smile of

Mona Lisa), could he have acted more than he had preached?

The use of our most important communication device, our skin, is a critical skill for positive self-expression. There are a few simple tips below.

Be Now. When talking, when you believe that you stay "up in your head," count on leaving behind your listeners. Learn to ultimately yourself (and serve them) by dancing with their questions and their concerns here and now. Your understanding of your subject and how you can express it will flourish if you can hear it, grasp it, and act on it. The key? Be here, serve now!

Relax and make yourself free. Can you capture more cash and ideas in an open or a tightly clenched fist and relaxed hand? Stress shortens your life, lengthens it with calmness. It's your decision.

Feel more than that. The sensation is the secret to becoming more present. After all, when can you feel anything other than here and now when the only time is? So, if you feel in your stomach any butterflies, a neck pain, sorrow, rage, happiness, or even fear... Be thankful; you're still alive! Take a deep, happy breath and concentrate your intellect and energy on delivering your message efficiently.

Inspire. The motivational word comes from Latin and means "breathing of spirit." You will need to inspire yourself and others to take action to bring every idea into being. The easiest way to get started is to inhale more air. Remember what's happening to you and your message's strength and reputation. We are all wind instruments. The more air you use, the more power and feel you can resonate with your listener, just like a flute or tuba.

React less/react more. Reacting means "acting again," reacting means "responding again." The first is an automatic process often triggered by an old pattern of behavior, often forgotten. The second can start with the very same stimuli. Still, by incorporating a little conscious reflection, you can respond politely back to your creative target in a way that pushes your conversation and its potential forward.

Prove value, "treat your listeners in a way that shows you,' know that you don't understand who they are.' What kind of response and help do you get if you practice treating others with all the wonder and interest of a little child? Could this enhanced level of respect encourage creativity and finance to further your cause?

CHAPTER SIX

The Body Language Of Man to woman While in Love

Determine how you can be hard to tell if a guy likes you. There are few things more stressful than wondering if you're interested in the man you want. Is he just like you, or is he just friendly? Does the way you think of him think of you? When you have a crush or are drawn to somebody, there are always so many questions. Luckily, there are several ways to say if a man likes you, and most of them are based on the body's language.

They send off several physical signals when guys are drawn to somebody. Some of them are deliberate, but most are unconscious. It means that you can often tell if a guy likes you is even aware of it, and the more a guy likes you, the more noticeable these signals will be.

Each of these indications expresses interest, nervousness, or appeal. Many people are representing all three. They say little by themselves. So if you find just one or two of these characteristics, you shouldn't take it as a sure sign that you're interested in the person you're talking about. Though, if you note that he often shows a lot of these characteristics when you're around or with you, there's a good chance he'll do like you. When you find these characteristics in a guy you like on an ongoing basis, you may want to show more interest in him. Often we are even more frustrated with guys than we are with them.

Body Language shows that when he sees you, he smiles. As women, when they know the man they like, they can't help smiling at all times. If you walk into the room, it seems to light up, and he might be interested in you. There's always a chance he likes you as a friend with a friendly smile, but it usually means something.

He's facing you. Instinctively, people turn to the things they care about. If he always seems to meet you or turns his body toward you even when facing back, there's a good chance he's interested in you.

He also smiles at you. He will look to you both consciously and unconsciously when a guy likes you to gauge your reaction to things. Even while speaking to you, he will be more likely to make eye contact with you often, though it's hard to tell if a guy looks at you because he's just interested in you. After all, you're in his line of sight. One way of saying this is to remember what he is doing if you catch him staring at you. If he's laughing or looking away quickly, you can almost bet he's been staring at you.

He's dilating his eyes. This one is always difficult to see because to note, and you need to be next to him. However, if you are sitting or standing close together, remember if his pupils appear more extensive than average. While some guys have larger or smaller eyes, most of them will show the difference when they look at someone they're drawn to.

He looks nervous. Do you know you're getting the antsy, jumpy feeling when you're talking to or just being close to the guy you like? He also feels like chances. It's as likely that guys will be nervous about a girl they want as we'll be nervous about them. There are some telltale signs of nervousness fidgeting, nervously looking around, and sweaty palms. While you may not always be able to rub off his hands on the side of his pants to dry them when a man sweaty palms, you might catch him subconsciously rubbing them off.

He's imitating you. When we like somebody, we appear to mimic them unconsciously. We're going to change our bodies to mirror the person we love. When you find the guy places his body to mimic yours regularly, it may be because he's interested in you. This is incredibly helpful when someone else is talking in group situations. Try crossing your arms or touching your face to test if a guy is paying attention to you. If he does it too, then you know he will probably pay more attention to you.

He seems to be exaggerating small gestures. We unconsciously do little things in an exaggerated way when we want to be heard. If you find that he appears to be making a show of small gestures like changing his cap, straightening his tie, or any other trivial detail, it might be because he is deliberately trying to get your attention.

He's rubbing the skin. Both guys and girls touch their hair or clothes instinctively when they like a person around them. It is due to the unconscious perception that it looks desirable and is often referred to as preening. While this may be a sign of vanity, it can also mean that he likes you and wants to look good because you love him, as well.

When he's around you, he crosses his face a lot. If you talk to a man and see him touching his face frequently, it might mean he's attracted to you. The attraction appears to enhance our senses, the sensation of touch most notably. This leads us to touch our faces instinctively.

He's holding you. He'll go out of his way to touch you when a guy likes you. This can be as subtle as scratching your fingertips as you offer something or as blatant as rubbing your leg as you talk to you. While some people are naturally inclined to touch others, most people will only affect you when they feel very relaxed and drawn to you. When, mainly when you're alone, he tends to go out of his way to reach you, it's almost sure that he likes you.

Whether you are not always easy to tell, these signs and signs will give you a good starting point. If a guy you want shows you three or more of these signals regularly, he's more likely to like you than not.

Rules of Business Body Language

The principles you keep in mind and never forget are known as the still applicable Golden rules. We shine brightly like torches to guide us in the dark of night to follow us on track and always propelling in the right direction.

There are golden rules for getting used to, faithfully observing, and teaching you why. Regardless of your primary purpose or what obstacle you face, the principle is to hold on when you start veering off course. Only seek and abide by the Golden Rule that applies. The principles you keep in mind and never forget are known as the still applicable Golden rules. We shine brightly like torches to guide us in the dark of night to follow us on track and always propelling in the right direction. There are golden rules for getting used to, faithfully observing, and teaching you why. Regardless of your primary purpose or what obstacle you face, the principle is to hold on when you start veering off course. Only seek and abide by the Golden Rule that applies.

The 5 Golden Business Body Language Rules are listed here.

Rule 1

People tend to lean forward and "with you" when they are interested in what you present, tell, suggest, etc. The explanation behind this is that we are unconsciously moving towards what we like. So, take a quick second to check your body language when you're interested in something someone is saying. You may find that you are leaning forward and being happily active. If fascinating or captivating things occur, the next time you're at a conference, exhibition, or lecture, look around at other participants. Next time you sell your product/service or offer a good idea to a potential customer, this experience will benefit you.

Rule 2

We are concerned when the shoulder blades of a man are not in line with your own. Have you ever been talking to a person talking to you, but their body seems to be facing you as if they will move past you?

First of all, giving them cognitive credit for speaking to you while concentrating on their next meeting, task, errand, etc. Remember, they probably mean well, but there's something in their mind's back (or front) that makes them nervous about riding.

It often happens when you happen to catch someone somewhere on their way and missed having a couple of words with you. If this occurs at a networking event or a one-sales presentation, you may need to use your smooth gift to help them focus entirely on what you're doing. Note that their shoulders are in line with yours when you talk.

Rule 3

Folded guns. This may indicate an anxious person's feeling uncomfortable. When they calculate, many people wrap their arms, weigh the facts, and don't feel confident about the answers.

This could be because you say something, the way you say it, or even a general mistrust of you by a person. You may need to know each other a little better and build confidence, not to be taken as an offense. If it's the same with a person you know reasonably well, it's probably the first reason or just a general sense of discomfort.

Rule 4

Two people are talking parallel to their shoulder blades. Have you ever been in business and seen two people talking in perfect alignment with their shoulder blades? This is a good indication that a severe or interesting conversation involves them. At least temporarily, the aligned shoulder blades say they close the doors to interrupt.

Note that their shoulder blades and general location of their bodies tend to face an exciting direction when the same discussion comes to an end. It occurs before the end of the conversation. It's a warning to proceed now without being disruptive when you're out at company networking events.

Rule 5

People are facing you absolutely, but they often look away. Usually, when a person is fully engaged in a subject, this is expressed in all elements of their being. The same happens in speech. Look at your next few interactions with the man. Should they give you regular contact with the eye?

Usually, when they don't look at you in the eye, they will say something that indicates listening or interacting. They're concerned if they're always looking over your shoulder or into the background.

Also, don't be insulted; remember this and, if possible, pick up the talk at a different time. This also depends on the talk's priority level. You're going to want to carefully start this and not offend anyone as you shorten the discussion.

You should trust these Golden Rules and believe them to help you understand the language of the business body better. They were tested over time

148

and proved to be accurate as well. Follow them carefully, and your ultimate success and your interactions will probably be much higher.

Would like you to know more about the language and networking of the business? I just finished my brand new Professional Networking Success Guide.

How Body Language Can Help to Restore Trust After Infidelity

People also know intuitively that the language of the body will encourage others to trust or mistrust you. But few people know how important it can be when a cheating spouse wants to determine whether or not the person who cheated them tells the truth. Don't make a mistake. They notice every expression of the face, every gesture, and all that you say without speaking. The chapter will explain how your body language can either help restore faith or indicate that you are still deceptive or not trustworthy.

My goal is not to make someone to cheat on their partner or hide things from them. My goal is to support severe people who would do anything to save their relationship, who are utterly over the affair, and who only want to be with their spouse (but can't get their spouse to believe these things.)

Eye Contact Is Difficult, But Vital: It can be complicated to look directly into the eyes of your partner if you betray them. You know you're wrong. You know you've caused them a lot of pain, and you can hardly stand to see all this right back at you.

However, this is precisely what you have to do, as hard as it is to see and face up to these things. When you can't look at your partner, they'll wonder precisely why. You don't want to spot a lie for them? Can't you be able to look at them because they're going to see the facts and you can't find them attractive anymore? Whether that's real or not, they're going to think about that. A cheated person is full of fear, distrust, and doubt. Often they'll look for clues as to why they're in this awful position now. When you can't see them in your face, what kind of message do you send?

I often tell people that if they can't stay in touch with their eyes, they should wait to talk. And you erode the trust every time you look back. A friend or spouse will naturally assume that when you look at them, you either have something to hide or you don't like what you see.

The Wide Open Stance: Another essential thing to remember is that you want to be open as it makes you look honest. Don't get your arms crossed. Don't rub your shoulders. If you are sitting, don't pass your legs. Put your hand on their back if your partner allows you to reach in and take their side. It's essential to lean back. This means you want to be next to them, and you want to cross your personal space to do it.

Always be mindful of how you sit, lean, and look. You never want a guarded or closed appearance. You still want to be open and sincere. If they permit it, you can try to touch them when you deliver some message. It means being honest and compassionate. There's a fine line here, though. You don't want to violate your personal space too much because this means you're going over your limits, being pushy, and trying to manipulate them to do something they're not doing comfortably right now. There is a big difference between positive, caring gestures and the body's language and gestures that are too deceptive and too soon pushy.

A brush of the hand, a palm on the back, grasping their shoulder can all be OK if they're relaxed with it, but a sincere hug or seeing how far they're going to let you go is often not the right thing to do so early. Begin by providing just the right, friendly touch, see if it is accepted and reciprocated, and then go from there.

It's so important you know not just your body language, but theirs as well. It will help you guestimate if you're too powerful or better off, giving them some time to process it before you deliver the message they're not yet ready to receive. Nothing dishonest with becoming honest and telling you hope they want some time for themselves, but you're entirely willing to offer anything they need when they're ready to accept it or want it.

CONCLUSION

The temperature drops when we're nervous or afraid. The temperature rises if we are comfortable and sexually aroused. During the more intimate stages of a sexual encounter, discomfort, or disapproval. It is also likely that emotionally cold people will be physically meaningful. If a man or woman is described as "hot stuff" or we're talking about a "warm embrace," it may be right. As they become more enthusiastic "cold men," they get hot, and their partner reads it-correctly-as; they also reveal their emotional state.

Hand's head caresses. Typically, before men, women tend to reach the top. Hand caressing head indicates increased confidence between two people as heads are extremely vulnerable-only those we feel close to can touch without us jumping or protesting.

CPSIA information can be obtained
at www.ICGtesting.com
Printed in the USA
LVHW021126210121
676969LV00005B/596